Sunset
Salad Book

By the Editors of Sunset Books
and Sunset Magazine

LANE BOOKS · MENLO PARK, CALIFORNIA

About Salads

A salad can introduce a meal, complement a meal, end a meal, or even *be* the meal. Salads take many different forms, varying all the way from green salads and vegetable salads to meat, seafood, and poultry salads; egg, cheese, rice, and paste salads; fruit salads; molded and frozen salads. Each one is a personal design which reflects the inventive genius of the cook.

Even the simplest of salads must be prepared with loving care and attention to details if it is to be a success. A simple tossed green salad is a gourmet's favorite, but simple as it may appear, it is by no means a haphazard creation. The greens must be fresh and crisp. The dressing must be a perfect blend of seasonings, selected to make the salad distinctive and to complement the meal with which it is to be served.

The recipes in this book include classic salads and variations of old favorites, plus many new and unusual salad and dressing recipes. You will probably find numerous recipes that you will wish to use without change, and others that you will want to adapt to your taste.

When you start to experiment with salads, marketing will become a new adventure. You will begin to select fruits and vegetables you've never tasted before and to combine foods you've never considered serving in the same bowl. Try different salad greens; there are many in today's markets, and you may find a new favorite among the more unusual ones you've not tried. Experiment with different vinegars or combinations of vinegars. Use herbs, fresh or dried, to transform your salads and give them delicious new overtones. By changing one or two ingredients in a salad, you can give it an entirely new character.

Salads take on excitement when served in eye-catching containers. Fruits are gloriously tempting when their rainbow colors are displayed on a handsome platter or on individual serving plates. Orange, pineapple, and melon halves make ideal serving baskets. Seafood salads become glamorous when heaped into lobster or crab shells. A handsome shallow bowl sets off color-bright chilled vegetables, and casseroles are ideal serving containers for any of the robust salads that replace a vegetable or an oven-baked casserole.

Garnishes give a salad its finished look. Give them special attention. A garnish can be as simple as a sprinkling of coconut, a wisp of parsley, or a topping of chopped nut meats, but it is important to the final picture.

First Printing June 1966
All rights reserved throughout the world. Copyright © 1966 by Lane Magazine & Book Co., Menlo Park, California. Library of Congress Catalog Card: 66-15337. Title Number 260. Lithographed in U.S.A.

Contents

Green Salads

VERSATILE AS THE GREENS THAT GO INTO THEM

A green salad, properly prepared, is an exciting addition to a meal; lack of loving care in its preparation usually results in mediocrity. Since no type of salad is at home in more menus than the versatile green salad, it deserves special consideration.

Strictly speaking, a green salad consists only of greens and a carefully seasoned dressing. If you add other ingredients, regard them merely as accessories; never let them dominate. Some additions that have special value for flavor or texture are sliced water chestnuts, green or ripe olives, capers, or herbs. Fruits and vegetables, either raw or cooked, may also be added to green salads; tomatoes, radishes, avocado, raw or cooked mushrooms, sliced raw cauliflower, orange or grapefruit segments, seedless grapes are but a few possibilities.

A tempting array of greens for use in making green salads is available in today's markets. You can choose from juicy dark green romaine, crisp iceberg, velvety butter lettuce, tender crinkled leaf lettuce, wispy chicory, and spicy water cress. Some of the most popular salad greens as well as some of the "accessory" greens, which add zest and individuality to a green salad, are pictured on pages 8 and 9. For some salads, you'll want to use a single variety from this selection, one that best complements the additions you plan to make to the salad. But when little or no accessories are to be added to a salad, it is best to choose a combination of two or more greens to give contrast in color, flavor, and texture.

HOW TO HANDLE SALAD GREENS

Always handle greens tenderly so they won't bruise. It is best to wash them the day before you plan to serve in order to give them time to chill and crisp. Wash greens quickly but thoroughly in running water. Remove wilted leaves, but do not separate the heads. Stand them upside down on a clean towel to drain for not more than thirty minutes; then gently shake off any excess moisture in a lettuce basket or towel. Wrap greens in a damp towel or put them into a plastic bag and refrigerate until chilled and crisp.

When serving time comes, pat off any excess moisture and tear the crisp, dry greens into bite-sized pieces. If you are making salad for a large group, you might tear the leaves an hour ahead and store them in large plastic bags in the refrigerator; otherwise, wait until the last possible moment to make your salad.

THE SALAD BOWL

Many different types of bowls can be used to make a green salad. Among the favorites of salad experts

Greek Spinach Salad is ready to toss; unusual ingredients include Feta cheese, fresh spinach and mint, cucumber, egg, and cinnamon. Recipe on page 7.

are those made of clear glass, plastic, and ceramic, as well as wooden bowls. A shallow bowl is best for green salads; it should be no deeper than about three inches so the leaves won't pack or crush.

Any bowl, even one of wood, must be washed to keep it from becoming rancid. Wooden bowls, however, should never be allowed to soak in water. The bowl, as well as the greens, should be chilled before you start making the salad.

HOW TO DRESS A GREEN SALAD

There are two basic techniques for adding the dressing to a green salad. One method is to make the dressing ahead in a jar or bottle; most of the special recipes that follow in this chapter are prepared this way. When using prepared dressing, pour just enough over the greens to coat all the leaves well; none of the dressing should drain into the bottom of the bowl.

One of the simplest ways to dress a green salad is the classic French method. When using this method, add the dressing ingredients to the greens, one by one—first the oil and seasonings, then the vinegar. The procedure is so simple and the rules so few that you can be adventurous in your choices of main ingredients:

1) Oil. Olive oil is popular for its flavor, but you can use your favorite vegetable oil instead.

2) Vinegar. White, rose, and red wine vinegars (some flavored with herbs) and cider vinegar are all interesting, or you may use lemon juice.

3) Seasonings. Salt and pepper are the only essentials, but you can add paprika or such fresh or dried herbs as basil, oregano, or tarragon, which can be grown in pots in the house or in the garden. Seeds like coriander, fennel, or mustard make good additions. Other choices might be crumbled Roquefort or blue cheese, toasted croutons, nuts, sesame seed, chopped green onion, chives, or garlic. A good way to add garlic is to rub the bowl with a clove of garlic cut in half.

The proportion of oil to vinegar can vary according to your taste. Experiment to determine your preference. The formula usually ranges from one part oil and one part vinegar to four parts oil and one part vinegar. Add salt to taste, or ¼ to ½ teaspoon for each ½ cup (8 tablespoons) oil.

Both vinegars and oils vary greatly, so the dressing should be tasted. If the vinegar is very acid, dilute it with wine, or use less of it. If the olive oil is strong, dilute it with a bland oil, such as corn or peanut oil.

If you wish to use a little showmanship, you can have the seasonings, oil, and vinegar on the table when you bring in the bowl of crisp torn greens. Sprinkle measured tablespoonfuls of oil over the salad greens, mixing until they are lightly coated with oil (for 3 quarts greens, you'll use 3 to 6 tablespoons oil). Season with salt and freshly ground pepper. Sprinkle measured tablespoons of vinegar over the salad and serve immediately.

To give you additional dressing ideas for green salads, several suggestions follow. Others appear in the chapter on Salad Dressings on pages 87 through 94. Each of the following recipes is for 3 quarts of greens. If you like a 2-to-1 formula, use 4 tablespoons oil, 2 tablespoons vinegar, ⅛ to ¼ teaspoon salt, and pepper to taste in each recipe.

Roquefort or Blue Cheese Dressing

Sprinkle oil over salad; mix. Season with salt and pepper. Sprinkle over 4 tablespoons crumbled Roquefort or blue cheese and red wine vinegar with or without garlic. Mix until ingredients are well blended.

Garlic Crouton Dressing

Put 4 tablespoons butter, 1 whole clove garlic, and 2 cups croutons in a frying pan; cook, stirring, over medium heat until croutons are golden. Discard garlic and have croutons ready in a bowl. Sprinkle oil over greens; mix. Season with salt, pepper, and red wine vinegar with garlic; mix. Sprinkle toasted croutons over salad, mix lightly, and serve.

Bacon-Onion Dressing

Sprinkle oil over salad; mix. Season with salt, pepper, ½ cup finely chopped chives or green onion, and 1 cup crumbled bacon. Sprinkle with red wine vinegar and mix.

Herb French Dressing

Sprinkle oil over greens; mix. Season with salt, pepper, and ½ teaspoon oregano and ½ teaspoon basil or 1 teaspoon tarragon. Sprinkle with basil vinegar or tarragon vinegar, and mix until ingredients are blended.

Onion and Water Cress Salad

Here is a special salad recipe that makes good use of onions.

2 large mild onions, peeled and sliced very thinly
   Cut clove garlic
2 bunches water cress
1 cucumber, very thinly sliced
   Thin red radish slices for garnish

SOUR CREAM DRESSING:

¾ cup sour cream
 2 tablespoons tarragon vinegar
½ teaspoon salt
¼ teaspoon pepper
¼ teaspoon dry mustard
   Pinch sugar

Arrange onion slices over bottom of salad bowl which you have rubbed with the garlic. Top onions with a layer of tender sprigs from the 2 bunches water cress. Arrange cucumber slices in center of water cress layer. Top with a dressing made by whipping the sour cream until smooth with tarragon vinegar, salt, pepper, dry mustard, and pinch of sugar. Garnish with radish slices. Mix salad to coat all parts with dressing. Makes 8 servings.

Green Salad with Cucumber and Buttermilk Dressing

Cucumber and buttermilk are used in the refreshing dressing for this salad.

⅓ cup buttermilk
 2 tablespoons mayonnaise
 2 tablespoons lemon juice
½ teaspoon dill weed
½ teaspoon salt
   Freshly ground pepper
½ cucumber (about a 4-inch section), finely diced
 4 to 6 cups broken pieces crisp iceberg lettuce

Shake together all ingredients except lettuce pieces. Pour over lettuce and mix lightly. Makes 4 servings.

Greek Cheese and Spinach Salad

This salad recipe comes from Greece, where Feta cheese originated. Feta is a clean-tasting, brine-salty white cheese sold in specialty food stores or Greek delicatessens. For another excellent but different salad, substitute the same amount of crumbled blue cheese.

1 pound fresh spinach
   Juice of half a lemon
2 tablespoons salad oil
3 ounces crumbled Feta cheese
1 cucumber, peeled and sliced
3 hard-cooked eggs, cut into wedges
1 tablespoon finely chopped fresh mint leaves
3 tablespoons salad oil
2 tablespoons wine vinegar
¼ teaspoon dry mustard
⅛ teaspoon ground cinnamon
   Dash of black pepper

Remove stems from spinach, carefully wash and drain leaves, and cut into 1-inch-wide strips. Put into chilled salad bowl, and sprinkle with the lemon juice and salad oil. Mix; chill for about 15 minutes. Arrange cheese, cucumber, eggs, and mint over top of spinach. At serving time, mix salad with a dressing made by mixing together thoroughly the salad oil, wine vinegar, mustard, cinnamon, and pepper. Makes about 8 servings.

LEAF LETTUCE

ROMAINE

AUSTRALIAN

CHICORY

BUTTER

WATER CRESS

HEAD

BELGIAN ENDIVE

ESCAROLE

Nine of the major salad greens available today: LEAF—Delicate taste; tender, fragile leaves, closely crinkled. ROMAINE (Cos)—Spicy mild, juicy; brittle-crisp, somewhat fibrous, clean-tearing. AUSTRALIAN (Oak Leaf, Salad Bowl)—Mellow flavor, slight bite; soft, suede-like leaf. CHICORY (Curly Endive)—Sprightly, rather bitter flavor; wiry, sharply feathered leaf. BUTTER (Boston, Butterhead)—Mild, almost tasteless; pliable soft leaf, velvety texture. WATER CRESS—Lively and spicy sweetness, sharp and biting; fragile, petal-like leaves. HEAD (Iceberg)—Icy bite, watery taste; unexcelled crispness. BELGIAN ENDIVE (French)—Lively taste, rich, mildly acrid; waxen, crunchy spears. ESCAROLE (Broad Leaf Endive)—Sharp, slightly bitter; rough textured.

Twelve "accessory" greens which add interest to salads: LEEKS—*Robust, strong aroma; mild, sweet oniony flavor.* FENNEL *(Anise)—Licorice sweetness; stalk and feathery top both used.* GREEN ONIONS—*Appetizing aroma; sweet-onion piquancy.* CHIVES—*Dainty and refreshing fragrance; refined onion qualities.* CELERY TOPS —*Nutty, spicy; sweet pungency, fragile tufts.* BEET TOPS—*Mildly sour, salty; young firm leaves.* DANDELION GREENS—*Tart bitter taste; thin, arrowy leaf.* MUSTARD GREENS—*Peppery-bitter; young, fully frilled leaves.* SPINACH—*Clean, "green" taste; tender young leaves, sharp edges.* NASTURTIUM LEAVES—*Peppery, somewhat like water cress.* MINT—*Fruity, refreshingly sweet scent; fuzzy leaves.* PARSLEY—*Acid sweet; slightly tough.*

Green Salads 9

Green Salad with Cantaloupe

Crisp vegetables and tart dressing are excellent contrasts for the rich cantaloupe in this salad. Have all the ingredients chilled and ready to serve; mix the salad just before serving.

 4 cups torn salad greens
10 radishes, sliced
 2 stalks celery, sliced
 1 small cantaloupe, seeded, peeled, diced
⅓ cup salad oil
 2 tablespoons tarragon wine vinegar
¼ teaspoon salt
¼ teaspoon chopped chives
   Dash pepper

Combine salad greens, radish and celery slices, and diced cantaloupe. For the dressing, mix together salad oil, tarragon wine vinegar, salt, chopped chives, and pepper. Makes 6 servings.

Fascination Salad

The fascinating thing about this salad is that in spite of the hot bacon-flavored dressing, the lettuce retains its crispness.

 8 slices bacon, cut in ½-inch pieces
 1 medium-sized head of lettuce
¼ cup chopped green onion (including some of the
     tops)
 2 hard-cooked eggs, sliced

Fry the bacon until crisp and browned. Drain, and use the drippings in making the dressing (recipe follows). Break lettuce into bite-sized pieces in a salad bowl. Add green onion and egg slices. Pour over the bacon dressing, mixing lightly. Serve immediately. Makes 6 to 8 servings.

BACON DRESSING:

Measure ¼ cup of the bacon drippings, and put back into frying pan. Add 3 tablespoons vinegar or lemon juice, 1 teaspoon sugar, ½ teaspoon paprika, ½ teaspoon dry mustard, ½ teaspoon salt, and a dash of pepper. Stir over low heat until hot.

Citrus Lettuce Salad

Some unusual ingredients, including orange and grapefruit sections, dates, and water cress make this tossed lettuce salad outstanding.

 1 head lettuce
½ bunch water cress
 1 grapefruit, sectioned
 2 oranges, sectioned
12 dates, pitted
¼ cup chopped preserved ginger
 1 package (3 oz.) cream cheese

Break lettuce and water cress into bite-sized pieces in a salad bowl. Add grapefruit and orange sections, dates, and ginger. Add just enough dressing (recipe follows) to moisten slightly. Crumble cream cheese into salad and toss lightly. Makes about 5 servings.

CITRUS DRESSING:

Combine in a covered jar ½ cup sugar, ⅓ cup vinegar, ⅓ cup catsup, 1 teaspoon salt, 1 small finely chopped onion, and 1 clove garlic (minced or mashed). Add enough salad oil (about 1 cup) to make 1 pint of dressing. Cover, shake well, and chill. Makes about 2 cups dressing.

Sicilian Green Salad

Sliced oranges and ripe olives add color to this salad. It's a good complement for a lamb entrée.

1 medium-sized head iceberg lettuce
1 can (2¼ oz.) pitted, sliced ripe olives
2 oranges, peeled and thinly sliced
¼ cup salad oil
¼ cup orange juice
2 tablespoons vinegar
1 teaspoon salt
½ teaspoon paprika

Break lettuce into bite-sized pieces and put in a salad bowl. Scatter olives and orange slices over greens. Mix with dressing made by combining the salad oil, orange juice, vinegar, salt, and paprika. Makes 4 to 6 servings.

Green Salad, Smörgåsbord Style

The idea here is simple: Bring the greens, the "go-alongs," and the Piquant Dressing (see page 89) to the table in separate containers. The dressing is added, the greens are mixed and served in individual bowls, and guests help themselves to a selection of the other ingredients.

In the picture on this page, equal parts of romaine, leaf, and Australian lettuce are used with small amounts of Belgian endive and chicory. Also included are pitted ripe olives stuffed with sticks of jack cheese, avocado cubes, halved artichoke hearts (preserved in oil), fresh mushroom slices, green onion pieces feathered on each end, and crumbled crisp bacon combined with halved toasted filberts.

You can use any favorite selection of greens that will give a good balance of color, flavor, and texture. Feel free to vary the additions with such things as toasted sesame seed, shredded Parmesan cheese, sliced water chestnuts or almonds, thin slices of apple, thin lemon curls, smoked oysters, bean sprouts, or croutons. Bring the crisp, cold greens to the table in a large separate bowl. Bring the other ingredients in smaller bowls.

Halloween Salad

Black olives and flecks of orange-colored crackers carry out a Halloween color theme in this salad. You may wish to omit the olives when serving it on other occasions.

1 head iceberg lettuce, crisped and torn
1 jar (6 oz.) marinated artichoke hearts
1 cup small cheese-flavored crackers, crumbled
3 tablespoons commercial Italian dressing
    Pitted ripe olives (optional)

Place lettuce in a salad bowl. Remove artichokes from the jar and cut them in halves; reserve ¼ cup of the marinade. Chill lettuce and artichokes in the refrigerator. Just before serving, sprinkle the crumbled crackers over top and toss with a combination of the marinade and Italian dressing. Top with a few olives, if desired. Makes 4 to 6 servings.

Green Salad, Smörgåsbord Style, combines several kinds of lettuce; other ingredients served separately.

Caesar Salad, Deluxe

This is much like Caesar Salad, dramatic to complete and serve at the table. Mandarin oranges, marinated artichokes, and avocado add interesting new flavors.

> 1 clove garlic, cut
> ½ cup olive oil or salad oil
> ½ teaspoon Worcestershire
> ¼ teaspoon dry mustard
> ¼ teaspoon paprika
> 1 teaspoon sugar
> ½ teaspoon salt
> Dash pepper
> 1½ cups crisp croutons
> About 2 quarts crisp salad greens
> 1 can (11 oz.) mandarin oranges, drained
> 1 jar (6 oz.) marinated artichoke hearts, drained and diced
> 1 avocado, peeled and diced
> ½ lemon

Drop cut clove of garlic into a ½-pint bottle or jar; add salad oil, Worcestershire, mustard, paprika, sugar, salt, and pepper. Let stand several hours. About 10 minutes before serving, discard garlic and pour oil mixture over croutons. Meanwhile break crisp greens into a large salad bowl; arrange mandarin orange sections, diced artichoke hearts, and the diced avocado attractively on top of the greens. Bring the bowl to the table; pour the oil and crouton mixture over the salad and mix in gently. Then squeeze the juice of half a lemon evenly over salad (strain seeds with tines of a fork). Mix the salad gently and serve. Makes 6 generous servings.

Caesar Salad

Caesar Salad is invariably tossed at the table, where everyone can watch the host or hostess season and mix the greens with a flourish.

> 1 clove garlic
> ¾ cup olive oil or salad oil
> 2 cups croutons (preferably made from stale sourdough French bread)
> 2 large heads romaine
> ½ teaspoon salt
> Freshly ground pepper
> 2 eggs, cooked 1 minute
> Juice of 1 large lemon
> 6 to 8 anchovy fillets, chopped
> ½ cup grated Parmesan cheese

Crush garlic in a small bowl, pour over the oil, and let stand several hours. Brown the croutons in ¼ cup of the garlic oil, stirring often. (If you prefer, you can toast the bread cubes in a slow oven.) Tear romaine into a large salad bowl, sprinkle with salt, and grind over a generous amount of pepper. Pour over remaining garlic oil and toss until every leaf is glossy.

Break the 1-minute eggs into salad; squeeze over the lemon juice, and mix thoroughly. Add chopped anchovies and grated cheese, and mix again. Lastly, add the croutons, mix gently, and serve immediately. Makes about 12 servings.

Semi-Caesar Salad

This salad dressing, similar to Caesar dressing, can be made ahead, but should not be stored longer than two days. Shake again just before using.

> 1 large head romaine
> 1 can (2¼ oz.) sliced, pitted, ripe olives, drained
> ¼ cup salad oil
> 1 egg yolk (raw)
> 1½ teaspoons Worcestershire
> 2 tablespoons lemon juice
> ¼ teaspoon pepper
> 2 tablespoons grated Parmesan cheese
> 1 clove garlic, minced or mashed
> 1 can (2 oz.) flat anchovy fillets

Ahead of time, wash the romaine leaves, dry them well, and refrigerate for several hours until crisp and chilled. Just before serving, break the romaine leaves into small pieces and put in a salad bowl, and add the olives. Into a glass jar with a tight-fitting lid, or into the container of your blender, put the salad oil, egg yolk, Worcestershire, lemon juice, pepper, Parmesan, and garlic. Shake the ingredients together in the jar, or whirl them in the blender. Drain anchovies well, chop finely, and stir into dressing. Just before serving, pour dressing over greens and mix lightly. Makes about 6 servings.

Frosted Lettuce Wedges

Garlic salt picks up the individual flavors of the creamy dressing that frosts these lettuce wedges.

1 teaspoon chili powder
½ teaspoon water
1 cup mayonnaise
1 can (6 oz.) tomato paste
1 teaspoon garlic salt
1 large head of lettuce

Dissolve chili powder in water, then stir into mayonnaise along with tomato paste and garlic salt. Beat until smooth and let stand 30 minutes. Cut lettuce in 8 wedges; frost with dressing just before serving. Makes 8 servings.

Water Cress Salad

Tender butter lettuce hearts and tangy water cress combine in this simple salad. It can be made ahead of time except for adding the dressing.

½ cup salad oil
⅓ cup tarragon vinegar
1 tablespoon orange marmalade
1 teaspoon salt
2 grapefruits , peeled and cut into sections
  Hearts from 2 heads butter lettuce
3 cups chopped water cress

Mix together oil, vinegar, marmalade, and salt. Pour dressing over grapefruit and chill for several hours. Break 1 lettuce heart into small pieces and mix with water cress. Line a salad bowl with leaves from the other lettuce heart; add water cress mixture. Cover and chill until serving time. Pour fruit and dressing over greens; mix and serve on chilled salad plates. Makes 6 servings.

Egg and Olive Lettuce Salad

Hard-cooked eggs and chopped ripe olives give a distinctive touch to this green salad.

1 head iceberg lettuce
2 hard-cooked eggs
2 tablespoons chopped ripe olives
2 tablespoons diced green pepper
1 tablespoon finely cut chives
¾ cup salad oil
¼ cup mild vinegar or lemon juice
1 tablespoon sugar
1 teaspoon salt
1 teaspoon paprika
1 teaspoon dry mustard
¼ teaspoon pepper
  Few drops liquid onion or garlic

Break lettuce in bite-sized pieces in a salad bowl. Press eggs through a fine wire strainer. Add eggs, olives, green pepper, and chives to lettuce. To make dressing, combine remaining ingredients and shake or mix well. Add dressing to taste. Mix lightly and serve. Makes about 5 servings.

Ripe olives and oranges accent the greens in Patio Salad, a perfect complement for barbecued steak.

Patio Salad

Crisp greens and peppery water cress are the base of this refreshing combination of oranges, sweet onions, olives, and a cooling herb dressing.

1 large sweet or mild-flavored onion
¼ cup vinegar
2 quarts crisp broken salad greens
2 cups chopped water cress
3 or 4 oranges, peeled and thinly sliced
1 cup pitted ripe olives, cut in half lengthwise
2 tablespoons finely chopped fresh mint
2 tablespoons finely chopped fresh parsley
½ cup salad oil or olive oil
¼ cup lime juice
2 tablespoons honey
2 teaspoons minced fresh or crumbled dried basil
¼ teaspoon paprika
    Dash cayenne
    Salt to taste

Thinly slice onion into a bowl and over it pour the vinegar. Let stand for about an hour; drain. Meanwhile, in a large bowl lightly mix salad greens with chopped water cress. On greens arrange sliced oranges, onion rings (drain off vinegar), and olives. Sprinkle with the mint and parsley. Combine salad oil, lime juice, honey, basil, paprika, cayenne, and salt. Pour over salad and mix well. Serve at once. Makes 6 to 8 servings.

Butter Lettuce Hearts with Gorgonzola Dressing

You can make this salad well ahead of time. It makes a good first course for a steak dinner.

⅔ cup olive oil or salad oil
¼ cup lemon juice
½ cup coarsely crumbled Gorgonzola cheese
½ teaspoon salt
¼ teaspoon black pepper
    Butter lettuce to make 6 cups bite-sized pieces

Shake oil with lemon juice, cheese, salt, and pepper. Cover and let stand at room temperature for several hours. Break lettuce into bite-sized pieces. Chill, covered, until ready to serve, then mix with the prepared dressing and spoon onto chilled salad plates. Makes 6 servings.

Summer Salad

This crisp green salad serves well in all situations— as a light lunch, a first course, or an accompaniment for a dinner or supper menu.

2 cups finely sliced fresh spinach
1½ cups sliced peeled cucumbers
⅓ cup sliced green onions, including some of the
    tops
½ cup sliced radishes
1 pint (2 cups) creamed cottage cheese
1 cup sour cream
2 teaspoons lemon juice
½ teaspoon salt
    Freshly ground pepper
    Parsley and paprika for garnish

In a bowl combine spinach, cucumbers, green onions, and radishes; mix together lightly. Arrange on 4 individual salad plates or in wooden salad bowls. In center of each serving, place a mound of cottage cheese. Blend together sour cream, lemon juice, salt, and pepper, and pour over salads. Sprinkle top of each salad with a little paprika and chopped parsley. Makes 4 servings.

Green Goddess Salad

This famous salad was first created in 1915 at the Palace Hotel in honor of George Arliss, who was appearing in San Francisco that year in William Archer's play, "The Green Goddess." There are many variations of the creamy dressing. Some cooks use sour cream for part of the mayonnaise or anchovy paste instead of the fish fillets. Others use a blender to chop together the parsley, tarragon, chives, and anchovy fillets. French dressing may be used instead of the vinegar.

Green Goddess Salad with lobster garnish is an especially rich version of plain green salad.

8 to 10 anchovy fillets
1 green onion
¼ cup minced parsley
2 tablespoons minced fresh tarragon or 1 tablespoon dried tarragon soaked in vinegar and then strained
¼ cup finely cut chives
3 cups mayonnaise
¼ cup tarragon vinegar
1 clove garlic
1 large head romaine
1 pound cooked lobster, shrimp, crab meat, or chicken

Chop together the anchovies and green onion until finely minced. Add parsley, tarragon, and chives, and mix lightly. Turn into a bowl and stir in mayonnaise and vinegar, mixing well. Rub a salad bowl with 1 cut clove of garlic and break romaine into bite-sized pieces into the bowl.

Pour over enough dressing to moisten (about 2 cups), mix lightly, spoon on salad plates, and garnish with desired shellfish or chicken. Makes 6 servings (Recipe makes about 1 quart dressing, or enough for 12 servings; you can store the leftover dressing in a covered container in the refrigerator for at least a week.)

Creamy Lettuce Salad

For luncheon you might serve this salad with rye bread and cheese sandwiches. As a dinner salad, its flavor would go well with steak, lamb chops, or fried chicken.

2 small heads iceberg lettuce or 2 quarts of leaf lettuce
6 slices bacon
1 tablespoon flour
1 cup (½ pint) sour cream
2 tablespoons vinegar
2 teaspoons sugar
1 teaspoon salt

Wash the lettuce and drain well; break into a large salad bowl. Cut the bacon into small pieces and fry until crisp and browned. Add flour to the bacon and drippings, and stir over low heat until flour is well blended. Add sour cream, vinegar, sugar, and salt; stir constantly until mixture is a smooth, thin sauce. Pour over the lettuce. Mix lightly and serve at once. Makes 6 to 8 servings when used as a dinner salad.

Spinach and Bacon Salad

You will enjoy this crisp, green salad both for its flavor and its appearance. The thin, tangy dressing is slightly sweet, so you may prefer to serve the salad European style as a separate course after the meat.

2 pounds fresh spinach
2 heads red leaf lettuce or 1 head iceberg lettuce
½ pound bacon
¼ cup sugar
1 teaspoon salt
1 teaspoon dry mustard
1 tablespoon juice scraped from onion
⅓ cup cider vinegar
1 cup salad oil
1 tablespoon poppy seed (optional)
1½ cups large curd cottage cheese

Thoroughly wash and drain the spinach; break off stems and tear apart large leaves. Combine with the lettuce, broken in bite-sized pieces. Fry bacon until crisp; then cool, crumble it, and add to greens. For the dressing, combine the sugar, salt, mustard, onion juice, vinegar, and salad oil. Shake or beat well. Add poppy seed, if used, and shake again. Use about half of this dressing to mix in the greens. Add cottage cheese to remaining dressing; mix with salad greens. Makes 8 servings.

Spinach Greens Salad with Pine Nut Dressing

Chopped pine nuts add new flavor to this dressing for fresh spinach greens.

½ cup chopped pine nuts
¼ cup salad or olive oil
3 tablespoons tarragon vinegar
¼ teaspoon grated lemon peel
½ teaspoon salt
Dash nutmeg
1½ quarts broken pieces crisp, fresh spinach

Combine pine nuts, salad or olive oil, vinegar, lemon peel, salt, and nutmeg. Mix with spinach. Makes 6 servings.

Belgian Endive with Curry-Nut Dressing

This exotic salad uses the slender, white heads of imported Belgian endive. Make the special dressing at least an hour in advance to allow the flavors to blend.

1 teaspoon prepared Dijon-style mustard
1 tablespoon lemon juice
3 tablespoons salad oil
⅓ teaspoon cinnamon
½ teaspoon curry powder
¼ teaspoon salt
1½ tablespoons chopped filberts or toasted almonds
  Romaine, washed and crisped
  Belgian endive

Combine the mustard, lemon juice, salad oil, cinnamon, curry powder, salt, and nuts; let stand for one hour.

Arrange individual salads, lining the salad plate with leaves of romaine. Arrange split heads of endive on top of the romaine, planning on three halves per person if heads are small, one per person if heads are 2 inches in diameter and 4½ inches long. Makes about ⅓ cup dressing, enough for 4 to 6 servings.

Antipasto Salad

Anyone who has eaten in Italian restaurants is familiar with *antipasto*—those tempting morsels of such foods as salami, cheese, pickled vegetables, and anchovies that Italians traditionally serve as appetizers. Some of these piquantly flavored foods can be combined in a typical green salad.

The basic plan of an "antipasto salad" is simple. You just arrange a bed of greens in your salad bowl, then top the greens with a colorful array of any of the foods you might find on a tray of antipasto. Bring it to the table unmixed to show off the colorful arrangement; then mix with a simple oil and wine vinegar dressing. The result: a robust, first course salad for a summer dinner or a main dish salad to serve with a hot bread for lunch or a light supper.

For the greens, choose romaine, escarole, leaf lettuce, or iceberg lettuce; add a bit of chicory or dandelion greens, if available, for the sharp, bitter tang they contribute. Tear the greens into bite-sized pieces as you would for a regular green salad, or shred them. Either way, make a bed of crisp greens in a well-chilled salad bowl.

Let your imagination, your sense of flavor and color, and the contents of your kitchen dictate the assortment you choose for the antipasto toppings: canned tuna, drained and broken in chunks; anchovy fillets, rolled or plain; green or ripe olives, chopped or sliced; hard-cooked eggs, chopped or sliced; salami, shredded or cut in pieces; radish slices; green pepper, chopped or sliced; minced parsley; pimiento strips; chopped green onions; pickled artichoke hearts, halved or quartered; pickled mushrooms, sliced; Italian pickled vegetables, drained and chopped; fresh tomatoes, chopped or cut in wedges and seeded. When you've made your choice, arrange the foods attractively on the greens.

DRESSING:

To blend the hearty flavors of an antipasto salad, a very plain oil and vinegar dressing is best. You might try 1 part red wine vinegar with 3 parts mild olive oil (this may be part salad oil). Use garlic-flavored vinegar or oil if you wish, or rub the salad bowl with a cut clove of garlic before you begin. Add the dressing and mix the salad just before serving.

Green Salad With Shrimp

If you prefer, use an oil and vinegar dressing instead of the vinegar and sugar in this Philippine salad.

2 medium-sized heads iceberg lettuce, *washed and crisped*
4 hard-cooked eggs, *shelled and sliced*
    About 1 cup small cooked shrimp
8 green onions, *thinly sliced (including some of the tops)*
⅔ cup white or cider vinegar
3 to 4 teaspoons sugar
    Salt and pepper

Shred lettuce or break into small pieces and place in a salad bowl. Arrange on top of the lettuce, in alternating rows, the eggs, shrimp, and green onions until all are used. Mix vinegar with sugar and sprinkle over the salad. Season with salt and pepper to taste. Mix lightly. Makes 8 servings.

Colorful antipasto ingredients are temptingly arranged on a base of romaine lettuce.

Orange and Cucumber Green Salad

Orange and cucumber slices dress up this salad.

*2 heads butter lettuce
3 large oranges, peeled and sliced, membrane
    removed
1 small cucumber, sliced (peeled, if desired)
½ red onion, sliced thinly, separated in rings*

DRESSING:

*½ cup salad oil
3 tablespoons wine vinegar
¼ teaspoon chili powder
    Salt and freshly ground pepper to taste*

Arrange whole leaves of butter lettuce in a large, shallow salad bowl. Tuck orange slices and cucumber slices among the lettuce leaves. Arrange onion rings in overlapping circles on top of the salad.

For the dressing, combine salad oil, vinegar, chili powder, salt, and freshly ground pepper. Sprinkle on the salad just before serving. Makes 8 servings.

Orange and cucumber slices tucked among butter lettuce leaves with onion rings overlapping on top.

Fennel Salad

This crisp salad uses thin slices of the raw fennel head along with the chopped leaves.

*1 large head fennel
½ head iceberg lettuce
½ cup finely chopped fennel leaves
3 medium-sized tomatoes, peeled and sliced
¼ cup garlic wine vinegar
½ teaspoon salt
¼ teaspoon garlic salt
¼ teaspoon pepper
½ cup olive oil or salad oil*

Cut the fennel head in half lengthwise, then thinly slice crosswise as you would slice an onion. Also thinly slice the iceberg lettuce. Combine sliced fennel, lettuce, and fennel leaves in a salad bowl. Add sliced tomatoes. In a jar or bottle, combine the vinegar with the salt, garlic salt, pepper, and oil; shake to blend well. Pour over the salad, mix gently, and serve immediately. Makes 4 servings.

Pineapple Wilted Lettuce

"Wilted lettuce" designates a green salad mixed with a hot dressing instead of a cool one. This recipe is a basic wilted salad, with the addition of sweet chunks of pineapple.

*1 bunch leaf lettuce (about 2 quarts torn lettuce)
⅔ cup pineapple chunks (fresh, canned and drained,
    or frozen and thawed)
4 slices bacon, cut into small pieces
    About ¼ cup vinegar
2 tablespoons water
¼ teaspoon salt*

Break lettuce coarsely into a salad bowl. Add pineapple chunks. In a frying pan, cook bacon until crisp. Add vinegar, water, and salt to bacon and drippings. Bring to a boil, stirring. Continue to boil for about 2 minutes, or until dressing is slightly reduced. Pour hot dressing over lettuce and pineapple. Cover bowl for about 30 seconds. Mix the salad lightly. Serve immediately. Makes 4 servings.

Lemon-Dressed Green Salad

A lemon dressing containing no oil keeps this satisfying salad low in calories.

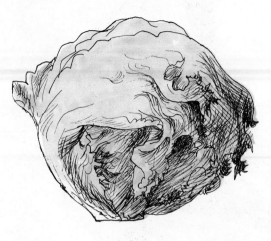

*1 small head romaine lettuce, washed, drained,
    leaves separated*
1 teaspoon sugar
¼ teaspoon salt
1 tablespoon lemon juice
1 tablespoon water
4 thin slices lemon

Arrange lettuce leaves in a salad bowl, cover, and refrigerate. Just before serving, sprinkle with the sugar, salt, and a mixture of the lemon juice and water. Toss and serve. Garnish with lemon slices. Makes 4 servings (10 calories per serving).

Wilted Lettuce
with Browned Butter Dressing

Unlike most wilted lettuce dressings, this has no vinegar. The tomatoes and onions in the salad give the desirable sharpness. The proper assembly and arranging of the salad is important so that you can pour the foaming browned butter dressing directly onto the green onions to cook them slightly before you mix the salad.

1 bunch leaf lettuce (about 2 quarts torn lettuce)
2 medium-sized tomatoes (cool, but not cold)
⅛ teaspoon salt
⅛ teaspoon pepper
*3 green onions with 2 inches of green tops, thinly
    sliced*
1 tablespoon sesame seed
5 tablespoons butter

Tear lettuce coarsely into salad bowl. Cut tomatoes into thin wedges, remove excess seeds, and place on top of lettuce. Sprinkle with salt and pepper. Drop onions in center of the salad. Meantime, in a small frying pan, heat sesame seed, stirring, until light brown. Add butter, allow to melt, and cook over medium heat until it foams and browns deeply (watch carefully; do not let it burn). Pour hot butter over onions. Mix salad lightly. Makes 4 servings.

Dutch Lettuce

This recipe violates the rule that salad greens should be broken, not cut; it calls for snipping the leafy greens into bite-sized pieces. The cut greens are part of the character of the salad.

Bacon, eggs, and sour cream thickly coating the lettuce make the salad so rich that a generous portion almost suffices for a salad supper. Smaller portions make a good salad accompaniment for simple meat.

1 bunch leaf lettuce
½ teaspoon salt
4 slices bacon, cut in small pieces
2 eggs
2 tablespoons sour cream
*   About 2 tablespoons vinegar*
1 teaspoon sugar
⅛ teaspoon pepper

With kitchen scissors, cut lettuce into salad bowl in bite-sized pieces. Sprinkle with salt. Meantime, in a frying pan, cook bacon until crisp. Remove from heat. (Remove any bacon drippings in excess of 3 tablespoons.) Beat together the eggs, sour cream, vinegar, sugar, and pepper. Pour into bacon drippings in frying pan. Over low heat, cook and stir until dressing becomes thick and smooth, of a mayonnaise consistency. Pour hot dressing over cut lettuce. Very gently mix to coat lettuce well. Makes 2 generous servings or 3 regular-sized servings.

Vegetable Salads

COLORFUL, CRISP, MENU-REFRESHING

A vegetable salad is a year-round, all-occasion menu refresher. It brings crisp freshness to a winter meal and delicious coolness to a summertime menu; it will perk up a family meal or round out a barbecue dinner. Some vegetable salads are hearty enough to be luncheon entrées, while others are elegant enough to spark up a party buffet table.

A vegetable salad, of course, can be only as good as the vegetables that go into it. Select good quality fresh vegetables and prepare them with care. Many vegetables which are ordinarily cooked make tasty salad ingredients when left raw; zucchini, cauliflower, broccoli, asparagus, and mushrooms are particularly good raw. When cooking vegetables for a salad, keep them on the tender-crisp side. Never let them get soft and limp, and drain immediately after cooking. Both raw and cooked vegetables should be chilled and crisp. If you wish to use leftover buttered vegetables in a salad, dip them in hot water or hot meat stock to remove the butter; then drain and chill. The stock will add flavor to your salad.

Use your imagination in combining salad vegetables, for many delectable combinations are possible. The only rule is to keep ingredients harmonious in color, texture, and flavor.

Salade Niçoise, tuna, and wine form a simple repast. Make this Mediterranean vegetable salad in advance for best flavor. Recipe on page 22.

Italian Appetizer Salad

This salad somewhat combines *antipasto* with greens. More than an "appetizer," it deserves an important place in the menu.

1 small head cauliflower
1 head red lettuce
1 head escarole
1 head curly endive
1 can (1 lb.) cut green beans
1 can (1 lb.) red kidney beans
1 can (1 lb.) garbanzos
2 or 3 green onions, chopped
6 hard-cooked eggs, sliced
1 cup olive oil
½ cup vinegar
1½ teaspoons salt
¼ teaspoon pepper
2 tomatoes, sliced
1 can (2¼ oz.) sliced ripe olives
1 or 2 cans (2 oz. each) anchovies (rolled or
  fillets)

Break cauliflower into flowerets and parboil until just slightly tender; drain. Combine in large salad bowl the greens, three kinds of beans, green onions, and 4 of the eggs. Mix with dressing made with oil, vinegar, salt, and pepper. Garnish top with tomato slices, remaining egg slices, olives, and anchovies. Serve immediately. Makes 10 to 12 servings.

Salade Niçoise

This mediterranean vegetable salad is at its prime when made in advance—a great advantage for the cook. Although considered a first course in France, it can be a complete, full meal salad. Don't feel bound to follow the recipe exactly. One of the joys of Salade Niçoise is its flexibility.

¾ cup olive oil
¼ cup red wine vinegar
¼ teaspoon salt
    Freshly ground pepper
2 tablespoons finely chopped chives
2 tablespoons finely chopped parsley
4 large boiling potatoes
    Boiling salted water
1½ pounds green beans
2 large tomatoes, peeled and cut in wedges
2 or 3 hard-cooked eggs, quartered
10 to 12 anchovy fillets
½ cup pitted extra large ripe olives
1 tablespoon capers (optional)
    Butter lettuce
1 can (7 oz.) solid pack white albacore tuna
    (optional)
    Water cress (optional)

For dressing, shake together oil, vinegar, salt, pepper, chives, and parsley; chill.

Cook unpeeled potatoes in boiling salted water 20 minutes, or until tender; cool immediately under cold water; peel and slice. Pour over just enough dressing to coat slices, mix lightly. Cover; chill at least 2 hours.

Cut off ends of beans and cut into 1½-inch lengths; cook in boiling salted water about 15 minutes or until crisp-tender; drain and cool immediately with cold water. Drain well again, then turn into a bowl and coat lightly with dressing. Cover and chill at least 2 hours.

Select a fairly deep platter or shallow bowl and mound potato salad down the center. Arrange marinated green beans on each side. Alternate the tomato wedges and egg quarters beside the green beans. Criss cross the anchovy fillets across the top of the potatoes. Garnish with olives and sprinkle with capers. Cover with foil or clear plastic film and chill until serving time. When ready to serve, add a border of the inside leaves of butter lettuce and pour remaining dressing over them. Arrange tuna on a side plate with water cress sprigs. Makes 4 servings.

Asparagus Salad

The old San Francisco recipe for Celery Victor (see page 26) inspired this luncheon salad.

2½ pounds fresh green asparagus, trimmed and
    washed
1 can (10½ oz.) beef bouillon
2 slices onion
1 carrot, sliced
1 bay leaf
½ teaspoon salt
½ teaspoon whole black peppers
    Romaine
    About 1 can (2 oz.) anchovy fillets
    Ripe olives (optional)
    Hard-cooked egg quarters (optional)
    Tarragon-Anchovy Dressing (recipe follows)

Tie asparagus into 4 bundles. Lay flat in a large pan. Add bouillon, onion, carrot, bay leaf, salt, and whole black peppers. Cook until tender, about 25 minutes. Lift from stock, chill.

To serve, remove string and arrange each bundle of asparagus on a salad plate with romaine; criss-cross 2 anchovy fillets on top of each bundle. Garnish plates with olives, egg quarters, and some of the cooked carrot slices, if you wish. Sprinkle with dressing. Makes 4 servings.

TARRAGON-ANCHOVY DRESSING:

Blend well 6 tablespoons salad oil, 5 tablespoons tarragon vinegar, 1 tablespoon finely chopped anchovies, ½ teaspoon dry mustard, 1 teaspoon sugar, 1 teaspoon finely minced parsley, 1 teaspoon finely minced chives, and ground pepper to taste.

Mexican Salad Bowl

Garlic croutons add crunchy bits of flavor to this mixed vegetable salad with a chili dressing.

4 slices bread, cut in ½-inch cubes
1 tablespoon butter or margarine
1 clove garlic, minced or mashed
½ cup sliced celery
½ cup finely sliced onion, separated into rings
½ green pepper, sliced
½ cup shredded carrots
1 cup diced cooked potatoes
1 head lettuce
⅓ cup salad oil or olive oil
¼ cup cider vinegar
1 teaspoon salt
Pepper to taste
2 teaspoons sugar
1 teaspoon chili powder
¼ teaspoon crumbled dried oregano
1 medium-sized avocado
Juice of 1 lime
½ cup stuffed green olives

Sauté bread cubes in butter with the garlic until bread is golden brown; drain on paper toweling. Mix together lightly the celery, onion, green pepper, carrots, potatoes, and the croutons; heap in a salad bowl lined with lettuce leaves. Blend together the salad oil, vinegar, salt, pepper, sugar, chili powder, and oregano. Pour over salad and mix lightly. Garnish the top with slices of avocado sprinkled with lime juice and with stuffed olives cut in half. Makes 8 servings.

Mexican Fiesta Salad

The name of this vegetable salad is suggested by its gay colors and the hot chili dressing.

1 head lettuce
1 large avocado
4 tomatoes, peeled and diced
1 green pepper, seeded and chopped
1 small onion, finely chopped
4 slices bacon
1½ teaspoons chili powder
½ teaspoon salt
⅓ cup cider vinegar

Line a salad bowl with lettuce broken into small pieces. Cut avocado in half lengthwise, pit, peel, and slice; arrange slices petal-like around the edge of the salad bowl. Pile diced tomatoes in the center. Sprinkle with green pepper and onion. Fry bacon until crisp and crumble over all. Stir chili powder and salt into bacon drippings; stir in vinegar and pour hot over the salad. Serve immediately. Makes 6 to 8 servings.

Bean Sprout and Water Chestnut Salad

Use fresh bean sprouts if you can find them for this salad; they are much crisper than the canned.

Clean sprouts well or drain the canned ones. To each 2 cups of sprouts, add ¼ cup sliced water chestnuts, ½ cup pineapple chunks, and ¼ cup slivered green pepper. For the dressing, combine 1 cup mayonnaise with 1 teaspoon soy and 1 teaspoon curry powder. Mix the dressing through the salad. Arrange salad in lettuce-lined bowl. Sprinkle toasted almonds over the top. Makes 6 servings.

Welsh Salad

Colorful rows of a wide selection of vegetables arranged on lettuce make this platter salad very handsome. The dressing is a light and low-calorie blend of cooling mint, parsley, lemon, and a little oil.

1 head iceberg lettuce, shredded
½ cup thinly sliced celery
½ cup thinly sliced radishes
½ cup thinly sliced cucumbers
½ cup coarsely chopped green pepper
½ cup coarsely chopped green onions (including some of the tops)
2 large tomatoes, thinly sliced
  About ½ cup pitted ripe olives
2 tablespoons finely chopped mint
2 tablespoons finely chopped parsley
3 tablespoons lemon juice
3 tablespoons salad oil
  Salt

Welsh Salad is a platter arrangement of fresh vegetables sprinkled with olives and dressing.

Make a bed of lettuce on a serving platter or chop plate. Arrange vegetables of each kind in a row over the lettuce. Scatter ripe olives over surface. Mix mint, parsley, lemon juice, and oil; sprinkle over salad, and then season with salt. Makes 6 servings.

Brussels Sprouts Slaw

Brussels sprouts can be used in place of cabbage to make a delicious slaw. Here they are dressed with a sour cream dressing.

2 pounds Brussels sprouts
2 eggs
½ cup sour cream
2 tablespoons melted butter or margarine
3 tablespoons vinegar
1¼ teaspoons salt
  Pepper

Wash and trim sprouts, removing the outside leaves. Place sprouts in ice water to crisp; drain thoroughly and cut crosswise in slices ⅛ inch thick; chill. Beat the eggs in a saucepan with sour cream and butter. Bring vinegar to a boil. Stirring, pour hot vinegar gradually into egg mixture; stirring, cook slowly until mixture is hot, but do not boil. Remove from heat, add salt and pepper to taste, then chill well. When dressing is cold, pour over sliced sprouts and mix lightly. Chill until ready to serve. Makes 6 to 8 servings.

Marinated Artichokes

You will need to prepare these marinated artichokes far enough in advance to allow them to stand at room temperature an hour or more.

6 medium-sized artichokes
  Boiling salted water
½ cup olive oil or salad oil
5 cloves garlic, minced or mashed
½ cup chopped fresh parsley
¼ cup lemon juice
½ teaspoon salt
  Dash of pepper
  Chicory or other salad greens

Wash artichokes thoroughly under running water. Cut off stems and remove coarse outer leaves. Also cut about 1 inch off the tops, cutting straight across with a sharp knife. Set in a large kettle with stem ends down. Cover with boiling water; cover pan and cook until tender, 30 minutes to 1 hour, depending on the size of the artichokes. Drain well and spread apart the leaves slightly. Combine the oil with garlic, parsley, lemon juice, salt, and pepper. Pour the oil mixture over the artichokes, and continue to pour through the artichokes until the leaves are well coated. Return artichokes to the pan and simmer them for 10 minutes in the oil mixture. Let stand at room temperature at least 1 hour before serving. Arrange on individual salad plates garnished with sprigs of chicory. Makes 6 servings.

Turkish Relish Salad

In Turkey, this colorful relish-like salad is a popular accompaniment for barbecued meats. You can shred the vegetables ahead and keep them well chilled. The ingredients are carefully arranged for attractive appearance, but the salad is mixed just before serving to blend the flavors thoroughly.

2 cups shredded cabbage
2 cups shredded carrots
2 cups shredded turnips
6 tablespoons minced parsley
2 teaspoons dill weed
  About ½ cup sliced pitted ripe olives
  About 1 teaspoon salt
2 tablespoons lemon juice
½ cup olive oil or salad oil
  About 1 lemon, thinly sliced

On a wide shallow serving platter, arrange cabbage, carrots, and turnips separately, side by side, to form three rows. Mix parsley with dill and make a band, using all of this mixture, around the outer edge of vegetables on platter. Delineate the rows of shredded vegetables by making a line of sliced olives between them. Sprinkle salad with about 1 teaspoon salt. Blend lemon juice with olive oil and drizzle evenly over salad. Garnish rim of platter with thin lemon slices. Mix salad, add more salt if needed, and serve. Makes 6 to 8 servings.

Shredded cabbage, carrots, and turnips are patterned colorfully for Turkish Relish Salad.

Artichoke Hearts in Tarragon Dressing

Prepare these artichoke hearts the day before, or early the day they are to be served, so they can marinate in their flavorful dressing.

½ cup olive oil or salad oil
¼ cup tarragon vinegar
⅛ teaspoon salt
  Dash pepper
  Dash dried tarragon
2 packages frozen artichoke hearts, thawed
  Crisp lettuce
  Cherry tomatoes
  Pitted ripe olives

Combine olive oil or salad oil with tarragon vinegar, salt, pepper, and tarragon. (If plain white wine vinegar is used, increase the dried tarragon.) Pour the dressing over the artichoke hearts and refrigerate several hours or overnight. Drain the artichokes and serve on a bed of crisp lettuce along with several cherry tomatoes and the olives. Makes 8 servings.

Celery Victor

Chef Victor Hirtzler of the St. Francis Hotel in San Francisco originated this now classic salad in the early 1900's.

2 small hearts of celery
1 medium-sized onion
2½ cups bouillon (10½-oz. can diluted with 1 can
*   water or 3 beef bouillon cubes dissolved in*
*   2½ cups hot water), or chicken stock*
1 cup well-seasoned French dressing
*   Water cress or shredded lettuce*
*   Coarsely ground black pepper*
*   Anchovy fillets*
*   Pimiento strips*
*   Tomatoes (optional)*
*   Ripe olives (optional)*

Wash celery, trim the root end, and cut off all but the smallest leaves. Peel and slice onion. Put whole celery hearts and sliced onion in shallow pan; cover with bouillon. Cover and cook until tender, about 15 minutes. Let cool in stock. Remove hearts, cut in half lengthwise, and place in shallow dish. Pour over French dressing (a garlic-flavored French dressing made with wine vinegar is especially good), and chill several hours.

To serve, drain off most of dressing and place celery on water cress or shredded lettuce. Sprinkle with pepper and garnish with anchovy fillets and pimiento strips. Tomatoes and ripe olives may be used for extra garnish. Makes 4 servings.

Anchovy-Broccoli Salad

This salad makes an especially attractive first course for a guest meal.

1 package (10 oz.) frozen broccoli spears
1½ tablespoons anchovy paste
1½ tablespoons finely minced green onion
½ clove garlic, minced or mashed
3 tablespoons finely chopped parsley
1 tablespoon chopped pimiento
2 tablespoons vinegar
2 teaspoons lemon juice
¼ cup sour cream or yogurt
½ cup mayonnaise
*   Dash of pepper*
1 head iceberg lettuce, shredded
2 medium-sized tomatoes, cut in wedges

Cook the broccoli as directed on the package. Drain, cover, and chill.

In a small bowl, a pint jar, or in your electric blender, combine the anchovy paste, onion, garlic, parsley, pimiento, vinegar, lemon juice, sour cream or yogurt, mayonnaise, and pepper. Whirl, stir, or shake until well blended.

Mound shredded lettuce on each of 4 salad plates. Arrange broccoli on top; garnish with tomato wedges. Shake or stir the dressing before spooning over salads. Pass additional dressing at the table. Makes 4 servings.

Aguacates Rellenos

Avocados can be stuffed with a mixed salad and served as an interesting part of a buffet supper.

1 cup cooked peas
1 cup cooked beans (lima or kidney)
1 cup cooked carrots
1 cup finely diced celery
½ cup French dressing
  Fresh garlic
  Salt
6 avocados
  Mayonnaise
  Finely minced parsley or paprika
  Lettuce for garnish

Combine peas, beans, carrots, and celery. Mix with French dressing, seasoned with a little fresh garlic; add salt to taste and marinate for several hours. Cut avocados in half, remove seeds, and peel carefully. Fill cavities with the vegetable mixture and top with mayonnaise if you wish. Sprinkle with parsley or dust with paprika. Serve garnished with lettuce. Makes 12 servings.

Frosted Cauliflower Salad

Mashed avocado, well seasoned, may be used to advantage to decorate a whole head of cauliflower which has been cooked and chilled.

1 head cauliflower
3 tablespoons wine vinegar
6 tablespoons olive oil
¼ teaspoon salt
¼ teaspoon pepper
1 small clove garlic
2 avocados
2 ripe tomatoes
1 onion, finely chopped
  Salt to taste
  Crisp greens

Cook whole head of cauliflower in salted water just until tender and no longer; chill. Shake together the vinegar, oil, salt, and pepper; drop in garlic and let stand in dressing until just before using. Peel and mash avocados, peel and dice to-matoes, and combine with chopped onion. Add salt to taste and whip together until fluffy. Place chilled cauliflower on chop plate, garnish with crisp greens. Pour oil and vinegar dressing over cauli-flower, then frost with avocado and tomato mix-ture. Makes 6 or more servings, depending on size of the cauliflower.

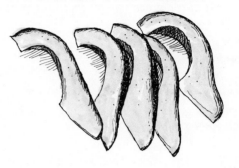

Tomato-Avocado Salad

The avocado mixture in this colorful salad re-sembles the Mexican *guacamole*, but without the flavor of chili. Serve the salad with broiled meat or fish for dinner, or with a cold meat sandwich for lunch.

1 large ripe avocado, peeled, seeded
2 small onions, finely chopped
  Juice of 1 lemon
2 medium-sized ripe tomatoes, peeled, chopped,
    excess juice drained
1 teaspoon paprika
½ teaspoon salt
¼ teaspoon pepper
1 large tomato, peeled and cut in 4 thick slices
  Crisp lettuce leaves
  Paprika

Mash avocado pulp. Combine onions with the mashed avocado and lemon juice in a bowl. Care-fully mix tomatoes, paprika, salt, and pepper with the avocado mixture.

Place each of the 4 tomato slices on a small bed of lettuce. Mound the avocado mixture on each slice; top with a dash of paprika. Makes 4 servings.

Celery Root Salad

Keep this salad in mind if you are planning a guest dinner, for it is one that improves when the celery root is marinated several hours or overnight. Be sure to buy firm, crisp celery root.

1½ to 2 pounds celery root
    Boiling salted water
 1 cup sliced celery
½ cup thinly sliced green onions, including part of
        the tops
¼ cup white wine vinegar
⅓ cup salad oil
½ teaspoon salt
⅛ teaspoon pepper
    Crisp salad greens
    Hard-cooked egg slices

Scrub the celery roots well, but do not peel them. Drop into boiling salted water and cook until just tender, 30 to 60 minutes, depending on sizes of the roots. When cool enough to handle, peel and dice the roots (you should have about 2 cups). Combine in a bowl the celery root, celery, and green onion. In a small jar, shake together the vinegar, oil, salt, and pepper; pour over the salad and mix gently. Cover and allow salad to marinate several hours or up to about 2 days.

To serve, line a salad bowl with the crisp greens. Spoon in the salad, and garnish the top with hard-cooked egg slices. Makes about 6 servings.

Grated Celery Root Salad

Serve this salad as a dinner first course or accompaniment.

 1 celery root, 1 to 1½ pounds
¼ cup sliced green onion
¼ cup shredded carrot
 1 tablespoon capers
¾ cup lemon mayonnaise (recipe follows)
    Red leaf lettuce

Peel celery root, removing tops and bottom; shred coarsely (you should have about 4 cups). Mix shredded celery root with onion, carrot, and capers. Blend in lemon mayonnaise. Chill and serve in a salad bowl lined with the lettuce. Makes about 6 servings.

LEMON MAYONNAISE:

Break 1 egg into blender container. Add ½ teaspoon grated lemon peel, ½ teaspoon dry mustard, ½ teaspoon salt, ¼ teaspoon oregano, 2 tablespoons lemon juice, and ¼ cup olive oil. Cover, and turn blender on low speed; *immediately* uncover and slowly pour in ¾ cup salad oil in a steady stream. Blend just until smooth. Makes 1 cup mayonnaise.

Cucumbers in Sour Cream

Thinly sliced cucumbers are dressed with a zesty sour cream sauce for this salad.

 3 large cucumbers
 1 teaspoon salt
 1 cup (½ pint) sour cream
⅓ cup mayonnaise
 1 tablespoon tarragon vinegar
 2 green onions (including part of tops), thinly sliced
 1 tablespoon finely minced parsley
 1 small clove garlic, minced or mashed
 1 teaspoon anchovy paste
 1 teaspoon Worcestershire
    Dash liquid hot-pepper seasoning
    Salad greens (optional)
    Chopped parsley (optional)

Pare the cucumbers if they have been waxed, or leave on the peel. Slice very thinly (you should have about 5 cups) into a bowl. Sprinkle with salt and let stand while you prepare sauce. Combine the sour cream, mayonnaise, and vinegar. Add the onions, parsley, garlic, anchovy paste, Worcestershire, and liquid hot-pepper seasoning; mix until well blended.

Drain the accumulated liquid from the cucumber slices. Pour the sour cream mixture over cucumbers and stir until blended. Cover and refrigerate at least 2 hours. Serve well chilled. You might garnish the serving dish with some salad greens and sprinkle additional chopped parsley over the top. Makes 6 to 8 servings.

Cucumber Salad with Yogurt Dressing

This fresh-tasting cucumber salad makes an excellent condiment to serve with a curry dinner.

2 medium-sized cucumbers
¼ teaspoon mustard seed
¼ teaspoon cumin seed
½ cup yogurt
¼ teaspoon salt
¼ teaspoon sugar
2 green onions, chopped

Slice the cucumbers very thinly; peel them if waxed. Grind the mustard seed and cumin seed in a mortar and pestle and add to the yogurt, along with salt and sugar. If you prefer, you can whirl all these ingredients in the blender instead of using the mortar and pestle. Mix the yogurt dressing with sliced cucumbers and top with chopped green onions. Serve the salad thoroughly chilled. Makes 4 to 6 servings.

Tarragon Cucumbers

A touch of tarragon and sweetening makes this salad unusually refreshing. If you haven't syrup from canned apricots on hand, you can substitute peach or pear syrup.

2 medium-sized cucumbers, peeled
1 teaspoon salt
⅓ cup fruit syrup from canned apricots
    About ¼ cup tarragon vinegar
1 teaspoon sugar
½ teaspoon fresh tarragon or ¼ teaspoon dried tarragon
¼ teaspoon freshly ground black pepper
    Salad greens
    Sliced cucumbers for garnish (unpeeled)

Slice cucumbers very thinly into a bowl. (The slicing section of a grater is a good utensil.) Sprinkle salt over cucumbers. Place a weight on top of cucumbers. Allow to stand at room temperature for 6 to 8 hours. Occasionally drain off the juice that collects. Combine apricot syrup, vinegar, sugar, tarragon, and pepper. Taste and add a little more vinegar if dressing is too sweet. About 1 hour before serving, pour dressing over cucumbers; mix lightly. Place in refrigerator to chill thoroughly. At serving time, turn cucumbers into chilled shallow bowl lined with crisp greens. Garnish, if you wish, with a row of unpeeled sliced cucumbers. Makes about 4 servings.

Scandinavian Cucumbers

Serve this cucumber salad as a first course.

4 large cucumbers, peeled and thinly sliced
2 teaspoons salt
2 teaspoons sugar
1 teaspoon dill weed
1 teaspoon chopped parsley
½ teaspoon white pepper
⅓ cup white wine vinegar
    Iceberg lettuce, cut in ½-inch slices
    Pimiento for garnish

You can use the coarse blade of a vegetable shredder to make uniformly thin cucumber slices; arrange them in layers in a bowl, sprinkling with the salt. Cover and refrigerate for several hours. Drain and rinse with cold water; drain again. Add sugar, dill weed, chopped parsley, and white pepper. Pour white wine vinegar over cucumbers, mix to blend, return to refrigerator and chill about 1 hour more. Drain and serve over iceberg lettuce; garnish with pimiento. Makes 8 servings.

Green Pea Salad

Prepare this company salad early in the day and mix in the yogurt or sour cream just before serving.

> 6 packages (10 oz. each) frozen peas
> ½ cup liquid, drained from peas
> ⅔ cup salad oil
> ⅓ cup red wine vinegar
> 1½ teaspoons salt
> 2 tablespoons crumbled dry or minced fresh mint
> 1 cup finely diced celery
> ½ cup yogurt or sour cream
> Lettuce
> About 4 tomatoes, cut in wedges

Cook frozen peas in a small amount of water until just heated through. Drain and reserve ½ cup cooking liquid; to this add salad oil, red wine vinegar, salt, and mint. Pour over peas, cover, and chill. (Do this early in the day.) Just before serving, mix in diced celery and yogurt. Spoon onto a large lettuce-lined serving tray or bowl and border with tomato wedges. Makes 12 to 14 servings.

Petite Pea Salad

This delicious salad travels well in a box lunch to a picnic site.

> 1 package (10 oz.) frozen peas with small onions, thawed
> 2 tablespoons water
> 1 sprig fresh mint, or ¼ teaspoon dry mint
> 2 or 3 thin lemon slices
> 2 tablespoons olive oil or salad oil
> 1 tablespoon vinegar
> Salt
> Lemon slices for garnish

Cook the thawed peas with small onions just until hot in water with mint and thin lemon slices. Remove from the heat and mix with olive oil or salad oil and vinegar. Add salt to taste; cover and chill. Drain dressing from salad and spoon into individual dishes. Decorate each with a fresh slice of lemon. Makes 3 servings.

An elegant dish for a buffet dinner, Green Pea Salad will serve twelve or more guests. Make it early in the day and chill; just before serving time, mix in the celery and yogurt or sour cream.

Zucchini Salad

Two advantages of this salad are that you prepare it ahead of time, and it makes an ideal accompaniment for barbecued meats.

  2 pounds small zucchini
    Boiling, salted water
¼ cup vinegar
  1 teaspoon salt
  2 teaspoons sugar
  4 tablespoons minced green onion
  3 tablespoons minced green pepper
  3 tablespoons sweet pickle relish
  2 tablespoons chopped parsley
  2 tablespoons chopped pimiento
½ cup salad oil
    Crisp salad greens

Scrub zucchini well; cut into thin slices. Drop into boiling, salted water and cook for 2 minutes. Drain well and cool. Combine in a bowl or a jar the vinegar, salt, sugar, green onion, green pepper, pickle relish, parsley, pimiento, and salad oil. Beat or shake until blended. Pour over cooled zucchini; refrigerate, covered, for at least 2 hours; stir gently once or twice.

At serving time, line a chilled salad bowl with greens. Spoon in marinated zucchini. Makes about 8 servings.

Green Pea and Cheese Salad

If you serve this hearty salad as a main dish, it makes about three servings.

¼ cup water
½ teaspoon salt
½ teaspoon sugar
  1 package (10 oz.) frozen green peas
¼ pound finely diced American or Cheddar cheese
      (about 1 cup)
½ cup finely sliced celery
  2 tablespoons chopped green onion
¼ cup thinly sliced radishes
  3 tablespoons chopped sweet pickle
⅓ cup mayonnaise
    Lettuce

Bring the water to a boil in a pan; add the salt, sugar, and frozen peas. Cover pan, and bring quickly to a boil over high heat; reduce heat and simmer 3 to 4 minutes. Turn into a bowl with ice cubes in the bottom. Cover and refrigerate until chilled. Drain peas well; add cheese, celery, green onion, and radishes. Combine the pickle and mayonnaise and stir into salad. Cover and chill about 1 hour. Serve on crisp lettuce. Makes 4 to 6 servings.

Kidney Bean Salad

Tender and mild kidney beans, in combination with crisp vegetables and a sharp dressing, make a hearty salad.

  2 cans (1 lb. each) red kidney beans, drained
  1 cup sliced celery
  1 green pepper, chopped
  1 dill pickle, diced
½ cup olive oil
½ cup red wine vinegar
¼ cup (4 tablespoons) chopped parsley
¼ cup (4 tablespoons) chopped green onions
½ clove garlic, mashed or minced
  1 tablespoon capers
  1 teaspoon minced fresh basil
  1 teaspoon minced fresh tarragon
½ teaspoon chili powder
  1 teaspoon sugar
    Few drops liquid hot-pepper seasoning
½ teaspoon salt
    Salad greens
    Sliced radishes
    Tomato wedges
    Freshly ground pepper

Mix together kidney beans, celery, green pepper, and dill pickle; chill. Just before serving, combine olive oil, wine vinegar, parsley, green onions, garlic, capers, basil, tarragon, chili powder, sugar, liquid hot-pepper seasoning, and salt; pour over salad mixture, then toss together gently. Arrange mixture on greens and garnish with sliced radishes and tomato wedges. Grind black pepper over salad before serving. Makes 8 servings.

Fiesta Hot Cabbage Slaw

The red and green of pimiento and pickle fleck this shredded cabbage salad, over which you pour a heated dressing with an especially fine flavor.

1 medium-sized cabbage, finely shredded
1 can (4 oz.) pimiento, cut in thin strips
½ cup chopped sweet pickles
¼ cup vinegar
2 tablespoons water
2 tablespoons sugar
¼ teaspoon salt
⅛ teaspoon paprika
⅛ teaspoon dry mustard
2 tablespoons olive oil or other salad oil
2 eggs, slightly beaten
½ cup whipping cream

Combine shredded cabbage and pimiento strips in a bowl with the chopped sweet pickles. In a saucepan combine the vinegar, water, sugar, salt, paprika, mustard, and salad oil. Heat to the boiling point. In a bowl, mix the eggs with the cream. Slowly stir the hot mixture into the eggs and cream, then return the entire mixture to the pan. Place over low heat and cook, stirring constantly, until slightly thickened. Pour, while still hot, over the cabbage mixture. Mix all the ingredients together lightly and serve immediately while still warm. Makes 6 to 8 servings.

Sesame Slaw

Toasted sesame seeds supply an exotic flavor to this cabbage salad. You can prepare the dressing ahead of time. Serve this distinctive dish with barbecued fish, poultry, or meats.

2 tablespoons sesame seed
2 tablespoons finely chopped onion (or 1 tablespoon
*   instant minced onion and 1 tablespoon water)*
½ cup sour cream
½ cup mayonnaise
1 tablespoon prepared mustard
¼ teaspoon salt
6 cups finely shredded cabbage

Spread the sesame seed in a shallow pan and toast in a moderately hot oven (375°) until golden brown, about 4 minutes; remove and cool. In a small bowl combine the onion (or instant onion soaked in the water for 5 minutes) with the sour cream, mayonnaise, mustard, and salt. If you make dressing ahead, cover and refrigerate.

Shortly before serving, combine the prepared dressing and toasted sesame seed with the crisp, finely shredded cabbage.; mix together lightly until well blended. Makes about 6 servings.

Turnip Salad

Turnips have a quality that is rarely explored. They change character, from sweet to hearty, according to the way they are seasoned. Here they are used raw, and teamed with sour cream and pickles.

2 cups turnips, cut in match-stick strips
⅓ cup sour cream
¼ cup diced cucumber pickle
¼ cup diced pickle
2 tablespoons brine from cucumber pickle
2 tablespoons brine from dill pickle
2 hard-cooked eggs, diced
*   Salt and pepper to taste*

Mix turnips with sour cream, diced cucumber and dill pickles, brine from each pickle, hard-cooked eggs, salt, and pepper. Makes 4 servings.

Southern California Fall Salad

The addition of fresh and dried fruits makes this otherwise unsweet cole slaw particularly appealing.

1 small head cabbage, chopped
6 small green onions, chopped
1 small green pepper (with inside pulp and seeds removed), chopped
1 medium-sized carrot, peeled and shredded
1 ripe pear, cored and diced
6 dried figs, diced
6 pitted, fresh dates, sliced crosswise
2 tablespoons salted cashews or peanuts, finely chopped
¾ cup mayonnaise (or more if desired)
2 teaspoons lemon juice

Place the chopped cabbage, green onions, and green pepper in a bowl. Add the shredded carrot, diced pear and figs, sliced dates, and chopped cashews to the first mixture and mix together. Combine the mayonnaise and lemon juice and mix in with the salad ingredients in the bowl. Refrigerate the salad a few minutes before serving. Makes about 6 servings.

Sauerkraut Slaw

This unusual salad can be kept in your refrigerator for several days. It is a colorful accompaniment to roast pork, fowl, fish, or wild game.

3 tablespoons white wine vinegar
½ cup salad oil
2 tablespoons honey
¼ teaspoon seasoned pepper or pepper
1 can (1 lb., 12 oz.) sauerkraut, drained thoroughly
3 tablespoons chopped pimiento
3 tablespoons chopped green pepper
1 stalk celery, thinly sliced
3 green onions, sliced (include part of the green tops)
1 teaspoon capers (optional)

Combine in a pan the vinegar, salad oil, honey, and pepper; heat, stirring until blended. Add the drained sauerkraut and continue stirring until heated through. Turn into a bowl and cool. Add the pimiento, green pepper, celery, onions, and capers, if used. Mix lightly until blended. Put into a glass container, cover tightly, and refrigerate until well chilled; it keeps well for several days. Makes about 6 or 8 servings.

Radish Snow Salad

Crunchy cabbage, mild cottage cheese, and lots of peppery chopped radishes provide contrasting layers in this salad.

4 cups very finely sliced red or white cabbage
½ cup garlic-flavored prepared French dressing
2 cups (1 pt.) small curd cottage cheese.
⅓ cup sour cream
2 tablespoons chopped green onion
2 tablespoons chopped green pepper
2 tablespoons chopped pimiento
Salt and pepper
1 cup finely chopped red radishes
Thinly sliced red radishes

Mix the cabbage with the dressing and arrange on a platter. Blend cottage cheese with sour cream, onion, green pepper, pimiento, and salt and pepper to taste. Spread cheese over cabbage and flatten surface with a spoon. Make a border of chopped radishes on top of the cheese and decorate with sliced radishes. Sprinkle with salt. Chill. Makes 5 to 6 servings.

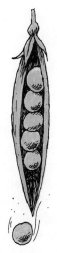

Cauliflower Salad

Don't overlook cooked, but still slightly crisp cauliflower as an ingredient for a delicious salad.

1 medium-sized cauliflower
Boiling, salted water
½ cup olive oil or salad oil
¼ cup white vinegar
¾ teaspoon salt
¼ teaspoon pepper
¼ teaspoon basil
6 anchovy fillets, diced
2 tablespoons capers
¼ cup sliced ripe olives
Salad greens

Break cauliflower into flowerettes, wash, and drop into boiling, salted water. Cook for 7 minutes or so, until tender but still slightly crisp. Drain, rinse in cold water, and drain again thoroughly. Put into a bowl. In another bowl or a glass jar, combine oil, vinegar, salt, pepper, and basil; shake or beat until well blended. Pour dressing over cauliflower. Add anchovy, capers, and olives; mix lightly. Cover and chill several hours or overnight, stirring several times.

To serve, lift the cauliflower with a slotted or runcible spoon, and arrange on the greens in the serving bowl. If you wish, serve the marinade as extra dressing to spoon over the salad. Makes about 6 servings.

Brazilian Heart of Palm Salad

Arrange sliced lettuce on individual plates; sprinkle with salt, pepper, a little lemon juice, and minced chives. Top each with half a peeled ripe tomato. Chop water cress, allowing ¼ cup (packed) for each serving, and mix with 2 tablespoons chopped heart of palm and just enough French dressing to hold together (use 3 parts light salad oil to 1 part lemon juice, salt, and pepper). Mound on top of each tomato and serve. (Water chestnuts may be substituted for the heart of palm.)

Eggplant Salad

Here is an interesting new way to enjoy eggplant. Combine it with bright red tomatoes to make a colorful and unusual salad. As an extra advantage, you can make this salad ahead of time and marinate it in the refrigerator for several hours.

1 medium-sized eggplant
2 green onions, chopped
3 medium-sized fresh tomatoes cut in cubes
¼ cup cider vinegar
3 tablespoons salad oil
1½ teaspoons salt
Freshly ground pepper to taste
½ teaspoon sugar

Wash the eggplant and set it on a baking sheet without peeling it. Bake in a moderately hot oven (375°) for about 45 minutes, or until tender when pierced with a fork. Peel when it is cool enough to handle; chill in your refrigerator. Cut the eggplant into cubes. Mix it with onion, tomatoes, vinegar, salad oil, salt, pepper, and sugar. Chill for several hours to marinate the vegetables. Serve on lettuce. Makes 4 to 6 servings.

Mushroom and Lima Bean Salad

Here lima beans benefit from chilling in a spicy French dressing marinade.

1 package (10 oz.) frozen lima beans
8 sliced fresh mushrooms or 1 can (4 oz.) sliced
    mushrooms, drained
1 large onion, chopped
1 tablespoon chopped fresh parsley or 1 teaspoon
    dry parsley flakes
½ teaspoon oregano
⅓ cup wine vinegar
3 tablespoons olive oil
1 clove garlic, minced or mashed
½ teaspoon salt
¼ teaspoon celery salt
¼ teaspoon pepper
    Onion rings

Cook lima beans according to package directions until tender. Drain, rinse under cold running water, and drain thoroughly again. Mix together with mushrooms, onion, parsley, and oregano.

In a covered jar or container, shake together vinegar, olive oil, garlic, salt, celery salt, and pepper. Pour over bean mixture and toss thoroughly. Chill in refrigerator 1 to 2 hours. To serve, heap into a bowl lined with crisp salad greens. Garnish with thinly sliced onion rings. Makes 4 servings.

Lima Bean and Olive Salad

Olives make a distinct contribution to this chilled bean salad.

2 packages (10 oz. each) frozen lima beans
¼ cup cooking liquid drained from beans
⅓ cup olive oil or salad oil
4 tablespoons vinegar
½ cup minced celery
½ cup minced sweet pickle
½ cup sliced pimiento-stuffed Spanish-style green
    olives
½ cup sliced pitted ripe olives
    Salt to taste
    Butter lettuce leaves

Cook lima beans according to directions on the carton. Drain, reserving ¼ cup of the cooking liquid. To this liquid, add olive oil or salad oil and vinegar. Pour over beans. Add the celery, sweet pickle, green olives, ripe olives, and salt to taste. Cover and chill. Serve in a bowl lined with butter lettuce leaves. Makes 6 servings.

Marinated Green Beans

Either fresh, frozen, or canned green beans can be given this treatment. Use mild, sweet onions, if they are available.

About 2 cups cut green beans
¼ cup liquid drained from beans
½ cup wine vinegar or cider vinegar
3 tablespoons sugar
½ teaspoon dill seed
¼ teaspoon caraway seed
¼ teaspoon salt
    About 1 cup thinly sliced sweet onions
    Crisp salad greens
    Tomato wedges (optional)

Cook fresh beans until just tender or cook frozen beans as directed on the package. Drain the cooked or canned beans, saving ¼ cup of the cooking liquid; turn the beans into a bowl. Combine the vinegar with the bean liquid in a small pan. Add the sugar, dill, caraway, and salt; heat just until the sugar is dissolved. Cool slightly. Combine the onion rings with the beans; pour the cooled vinegar mixture over them. Cover the bowl and refrigerate for 2 to 3 hours before serving. To serve, lift the beans out of the marinade with a slotted spoon and arrange them on crisp salad greens. Garnish the dish with fresh tomato wedges, if you wish. Makes 4 servings.

Deluxe Romaine and Potato Salad

This vegetable salad is a light, showy version of potato salad. At the table, you mix the attractively arranged ingredients with croutons and bacon, which are reserved until the last moment to preserve their crispness.

Dressing (recipe follows)
4 cups warm, cooked potatoes, peeled and diced
2 tablespoons chopped pimiento
6 anchovy fillets, chopped
1 large head romaine lettuce
¼ cup shredded Parmesan cheese
½ cup crumbled blue cheese
½ cup thinly sliced green onions, including some tops
3 hard-cooked eggs, cut in wedges
2 teaspoons drained capers
6 slices bacon, cooked and crumbled
4 cups croutons (recipe follows)

At the table, mix this Deluxe Romaine and Potato Salad with bacon, croutons, and capers.

Pour half the dressing over the potatoes and save the remainder. Mix pimiento and anchovies with potatoes; cover and chill. Stir the potatoes several times while they chill.

Line a large salad bowl with some of the romaine leaves. Break the remainder of the head in bite-sized pieces and place in bowl. Cover with cold potatoes (including dressing). Arrange attractively over potatoes the Parmesan cheese, blue cheese, green onions, and hard-cooked eggs.

Present the salad with the capers, bacon, and croutons each in a small dish of its own. Mix everything at the table, pouring in enough of the reserved dressing to moisten the ingredients. Serve at once. Makes 8 servings.

DRESSING:

Beat together 1 cup salad oil or olive oil, ½ cup white wine vinegar, 1½ teaspoons salt, and about ¼ teaspoon freshly ground black pepper.

CROUTONS:

Cut in cubes enough firm-textured whole wheat bread to make 4 cups. Heat ⅓ cup salad oil in a wide frying pan. Add croutons and brown evenly, stirring constantly. Serve soon, or store in an airtight container.

Danish Potato Salad

Prepare this salad ahead to marinate and chill until time to mix and serve.

4 medium-sized whole potatoes
Boiling salted water
1 clove garlic, split
2 tablespoons salad oil
¼ cup tarragon wine vinegar
1 teaspoon salt
1 teaspoon sugar
½ teaspoon dill weed
3 hard-cooked eggs, shelled
2 green onions, sliced
3 large radishes, sliced
⅓ cup mayonnaise
Chopped parsley for garnish

Cook potatoes in boiling salted water just until tender. Drain and peel; cut in ½-inch cubes while still warm. You should have 4 cups. Drop garlic into a jar with salad oil; let stand about 10 minutes, then discard garlic. Add to the jar the vinegar, salt, sugar, and dill weed; pour dressing over warm potatoes. Cover and refrigerate for several hours. Also refrigerate the eggs.

At serving time, mix into the salad the onion slices, radish slices, 2 of the hard-cooked eggs, chopped, and the mayonnaise. Garnish with slices or wedges of the remaining hard-cooked egg and chopped parsley. Makes 6 servings.

French Potato Salad

The tart, peppery seasoning in this salad distinguishes it from standard potato salads. Try it with steak in place of the traditional French fries.

Cook 8 small, round red potatoes in their skins until tender. Without peeling, slice potatoes thinly. Peel and slice very thinly one Bermuda onion; separate into rings. In shallow dish place alternate layers of the sliced potatoes and onion rings; salt and pepper each layer and sprinkle chopped parsley bits over it. Make French dressing with 2 tablespoons white wine vinegar and 3 tablespoons salad oil. Pour dressing over layers of potato and onion and refrigerate salad overnight. Turn mixture at least once to make sure salad is well coated with the marinade. Makes about 5 servings.

Tomato Salad

Make this salad two or three hours before dinner and allow to chill for best flavor.

2 pounds small, firm tomatoes, peeled and thinly sliced
2 onions (about same size as tomatoes), thinly sliced
½ teaspoon salt
  Dash cayenne pepper
¼ teaspoon Worcestershire
¼ teaspoon powdered sugar
½ cup red wine vinegar
¼ cup salad oil or olive oil

Alternate tomato and onion slices in layers in a bowl. Mix together the salt, cayenne pepper, Worcestershire, powdered sugar, vinegar, and salad oil or olive oil. Cover; chill about 2 hours. Drain off marinade. Makes 6 servings.

Stuffed Tomato Salad

This is not the usual stuffed tomato salad. Cubes of Swiss cheese, bologna, and potato blend with the zippy onion seasoning.

2 cups diced cooked potatoes
1 cup small Swiss cheese cubes
⅔ cup diced bologna
1 small onion, finely chopped
  Salt and pepper to taste
½ cup sharp French dressing
6 large tomatoes
  Mayonnaise
  Paprika
  Lettuce

In a large bowl, combine potatoes, Swiss cheese cubes, bologna, onion, salt, and pepper. Mix lightly with French dressing. Remove stem ends from tomatoes. With a sharp knife, slash from top halfway down each tomato in about 6 places. Spread tomato open. Fill with potato mixture. Top with a spoonful of mayonnaise and a dusting of paprika, if desired. Serve on lettuce-lined individual salad plates. Makes 6 servings.

Garlic Tomatoes

Chilled, garlic-seasoned, sliced tomatoes are an especially good accompaniment for barbecued shortribs, steaks, or hamburgers. Scald and peel 5 large tomatoes; cut in ⅓-inch-thick slices. Place a single layer of the tomatoes on a chop plate.

To 1½ cups French dressing, add 1 or 2 cloves of garlic, mashed or minced. Pour some of the dressing mixture over tomatoes; sprinkle with crumbled dried oregano, salt, and pepper. Add another layer of tomato slices, and repeat dressing, oregano, salt, and pepper. Continue until all tomato slices are used. Cover chop plate with foil and chill for at least 3 hours. Makes 8 servings.

Meat, Seafood, & Poultry Salads

HEARTY MEMBERS OF THE SALAD FAMILY

Meat, seafood, and poultry salads are the hearty members of the salad family. Often they are served as full-meal salads or as the mainstay of a luncheon or supper. In small servings, however, many of them make excellent appetizer salads.

You will find some famous salads in this group. The Crab Louis on page 50 has become a classic dish that is served in many restaurants; the Louis dressing is also used on other seafood salads as well. The Cobb Salad on page 43 is another old favorite, and on page 47, prawns are dressed with a version of the famous Green Goddess Salad Dressing, found on page 91.

Salads in this chapter make wonderful use of leftovers. Chunky bits of leftover chicken, for example, become impressive enough for a party luncheon when combined with mandarin oranges, pineapple chunks, and toasted, slivered almonds. Colorful apple slices and grape halves stretch leftover ham into a main-dish salad with delightful texture contrasts.

Most of the salads that follow have one thing in common: They combine crisp, crunchy ingredients—green pepper, cucumber, pickle, nuts, celery—to offset the smoother, heavier textures of meat, fish, and poultry.

Shellfish blended with fresh herb mayonnaise, served from marinated artichoke cases, makes a tasty main-dish salad. Recipe on page 51.

Knackwurst Salad with Mustard Dressing

This salad is as easy to prepare as it is delicious.

*4 German garlic sausages (knackwurst),
    casings removed*
¾ cup vinegar
½ cup salad oil
2 tablespoons mayonnaise
2 teaspoons prepared mustard
1 small onion, chopped fine
2 cloves garlic, minced or mashed
1 teaspoon salt
¼ teaspoon pepper
    Hard-cooked egg wedges
    Tomatoes
    Pickles
    Parsley

Slice each sausage in half lengthwise, then cut in diagonal slices ⅛ inch thick. Arrange slices in shallow platter in sausage shapes. Over them pour a dressing made by shaking together the vinegar, salad oil, mayonnaise, mustard, onion, garlic, salt, and pepper. Chill 1 to 2 hours. Garnish with hard-cooked egg wedges, tomatoes, pickles, and parsley. Makes 4 entreé-size servings.

Frankfurt Tongue and Potato Salad

A green mayonnaise, similar to Gribiche sauce, dresses the two meats and canned vegetables in this combination salad. The caper-flecked sauce is a specialty of Frankfurt, Germany, where it is used to embellish cold cuts and boiled potatoes.

Either cook a fresh beef tongue in advance for this recipe, or buy sliced tongue from a delicatessen. This dish goes together readily once the sauce is made.

2 cans (1 lb. each) vertical pack green beans, drained
2 cans (1 lb. each) whole new potatoes, drained
2 cans (1 lb. each) asparagus spears, drained
¼ cup olive oil or salad oil
2 tablespoons white wine vinegar
¼ teaspoon salt
¼ teaspoon dry mustard
8 slices cooked tongue, cut about ⅜ inch thick
8 slices boiled or baked ham, cut about ⅜ inch thick
1 bunch radishes, cut in rose shapes
Green Dressing (recipe follows)

Select a serving dish or baking dish about 8 inches wide and 12 inches long. Arrange drained beans, potatoes, and asparagus in the dish; place beans and asparagus at either end and potatoes in the center. Mix together the oil, vinegar, salt, and mustard, and pour over vegetables. Chill at least 2 hours. Just before serving time, alternate ham and tongue slices in a row across the top of the vegetables and garnish with radish roses. Spoon chilled green dressing over the meats and pass additional dressing. Makes 8 servings.

GREEN DRESSING:

Hard cook 3 eggs and let cool. Separate the egg whites and reserve. Mash the egg yolks in a bowl and mix in 1 teaspoon dry mustard, ½ teaspoon salt, and freshly ground pepper. Gradually blend in ¾ cup olive oil or salad oil, and 2 tablespoons lemon juice. Mix in ½ cup sour cream. Stir in ⅓ cup finely chopped parsley, ⅓ cup finely chopped dill pickle, 1 tablespoon chopped capers, 2 teaspoons grated onion, and the 3 finely chopped egg whites. Chill before serving. Makes 1 pint.

Tacos Salad

A warm meat sauce as a salad dressing may seem unique, but the flavors of this salad give you a clue that it is a simple adaptation of the Mexican taco, minus the fried tortilla.

1 head iceberg lettuce, shredded
2 green onions, chopped (including tops)
1 cup cooked or canned kidney beans, drained
1 hard-cooked egg, chopped
Meat dressing (recipe follows)
1 cup shredded medium-sharp Cheddar cheese or American cheese

In a salad bowl, mix together lettuce, onion, beans, and egg; chill while you prepare the dressing. Mix salad with the warm meat dressing, sprinkle with the shredded Cheddar cheese, and serve immediately. Makes 4 to 6 servings.

MEAT DRESSING:

½ pound ground beef
1 tablespoon salad oil
1 can (8 oz.) tomato sauce
1 cup beef broth (canned or made with beef stock concentrate)
¼ cup dry red wine or water
1 tablespoon instant minced onion
⅛ teaspoon garlic powder
⅛ teaspoon ground cumin
⅛ teaspoon black pepper
1 teaspoon chili powder
1 teaspoon salt

In a frying pan, break apart ground beef and brown with oil. Add tomato sauce, beef broth, red wine or water, minced onion, garlic powder, cumin, black pepper, chili powder, and salt. Simmer, uncovered, for 20 minutes. Let cool for 10 more minutes. Skim some of the fat off the sauce if desired, then combine with salad.

Beef and Mushroom Vinaigrette

Leftover beef roast, extra barbecued steak; or broiled flank steak make this salad a flexible supper entree. Lots of sautéed mushrooms and artichoke hearts dress up the herb-seasoned meat strips.

    1 pound mushrooms, washed and sliced
    7 tablespoons olive oil
      Juice of 1 lemon
    2 teaspoons chicken stock base
1½ pounds sirloin or flank steak, broiled and chilled
      (or leftover beef roast)
    ¼ cup dry red wine
    3 tablespoons red wine vinegar
    ¼ teaspoon chervil
    ¼ teaspoon thyme
    ¼ teaspoon basil
    ¼ teaspoon marjoram
      Salt and pepper to taste
    1 tomato, peeled and cut in wedges
    4 canned or cooked artichoke hearts

Sauté mushrooms in 3 tablespoons of the oil along with lemon juice and chicken stock base, cooking just until barely tender; let cool. Slice meat into ⅜-inch-thick strips. For dressing, mix together the remaining 4 tablespoons oil, red wine, wine vinegar, chervil, thyme, basil, and marjoram; stir in the juices drained from the mushrooms. Add salt and pepper to taste.

Arrange meat strips in a shallow serving dish and spoon mushrooms across the center of them. Place tomato wedges around the sides along with artichoke hearts. Pour over the dressing. Cover and chill at least 3 hours, basting several times with dressing. Makes 4 to 6 servings.

Skillet Frankfurter Salad

Reminiscent of German hot potato salad, this full-meal salad has a delicious sweet-sour dressing.

5 or 6 hot cooked potatoes, peeled and cubed
2 stalks celery, sliced
5 radishes, sliced
6 slices crisp cooked bacon, broken in large pieces
1 small head lettuce, torn in bite-sized pieces
1 cup cooked peas
  Hot Skillet Dressing (recipe follows)
3 hard-cooked eggs, sliced
  Crisp lettuce leaves

Mix potatoes, celery, radishes, bacon, and lettuce gently with peas and Hot Skillet Dressing. Heap back into the warm skillet. Garnish top with hard-cooked eggs and around edge with lettuce leaves. Makes 6 to 8 servings.

HOT SKILLET DRESSING:

    Boiling water
  6 regular-sized frankfurters
  1 small onion, finely chopped
  ¼ cup bacon drippings
  2 tablespoons flour
  1 cup chicken broth
  ⅓ cup vinegar
1½ teaspoons salt
    Few grains pepper
  1 teaspoon celery seed
  1 tablespoon sugar

Pour boiling water over frankfurters and let stand 5 minutes. Sauté onion in bacon drippings until soft but not browned. Blend in flour. Add broth slowly; cook and stir until smooth and thickened. Stir in vinegar, salt, pepper, celery seed, and sugar. Cook 5 minutes more. Drain the frankfurters, slice, and add to dressing.

Ham and Turkey Salad

This main dish salad combines cooked turkey and ham in a curry-flavored dressing.

  4 cups diced, cooked turkey
  2 cups diced, cooked ham (or cut in matchstick-
    sized pieces)
  1 cup toasted, slivered almonds
  1 large red-skinned apple
  1 tablespoon lemon juice
  1 cup halved, seeded grapes or halved, canned
    litchi nuts
1½ cups mayonnaise
  2 teaspoons soy sauce
1½ teaspoons curry powder
    Crisp salad greens
    Toasted slivered almonds, apple slices, and
      litchi nuts or grapes for garnish (optional)

Combine the turkey, ham, and almonds. Thinly slice the unpeeled apple and coat with lemon juice. Add apple to salad with the grapes or litchi nuts. Blend mayonnaise with soy and curry; pour over salad. Pack into a 2½-quart bowl, cover, and chill for several hours, or overnight. To serve, turn out on a bed of the greens. For garnish, sprinkle more

toasted almonds on top and surround with more apple slices (rubbed with lemon juice) and litchi nuts or grapes. Makes 6 to 8 servings.

Ham and Fruit Luncheon Salad

The typical chef's salad undergoes some interesting changes here. Along with the julienne strips of ham and cheese on lettuce, oranges and dried figs with a sour cream dressing add a refreshing tang and subtle sweetness.

  1 head iceberg lettuce, chopped
  4 slices Swiss cheese, cut in thin strips
  2 oranges, peeled and sectioned
10 dried calimyrna or mission figs, sliced
  5 slices boiled ham, cut in thin strips
    Sour cream dressing (recipe follows)

Place lettuce in a salad bowl. Lightly mix together cheese, orange sections, figs, and ham and turn onto lettuce. Pour over the sour cream dressing. Mix and serve. Makes 6 servings.

SOUR CREAM DRESSING:

Blend 1 cup sour cream with ¼ cup orange juice, 2 teaspoons sugar, ½ teaspoon paprika, and ½ teaspoon salt.

Pineapple and Ham Salad

If you have ham for dinner one night, plan to serve this salad later in the week.

    Salad greens, torn in bite-sized pieces
1½ to 2 cups diced, cooked ham
  1 can (13½ oz.) pineapple chunks, drained well
¼ cup chopped green pepper
¼ cup mayonnaise
  2 tablespoons sweet pickle relish
  1 tablespoon prepared horse-radish
  1 teaspoon prepared mustard

Line your salad bowl with greens. Mound diced ham in the center of the bowl. Arrange pineapple

Feature this Ham and Turkey Salad containing almonds, apples, and litchi nuts at a company luncheon.

chunks in a ring surrounding ham. Sprinkle green pepper in a ring between ham and pineapple. Chill until serving time. Meanwhile combine mayonnaise, sweet pickle relish, horse-radish, and mustard; blend together and chill. At serving time, bring salad to the table, add dressing, mix, and serve. Makes 4 to 6 servings.

Normandy Salad

Try this potato salad with ham for a luncheon main dish.

Peel and boil 2 pounds potatoes until just tender. Cool and cut julienne (in match-like pieces); you should have about 4 cups. Cut raw celery the same way to make equal amounts of the two vegetables. Salt and pepper to taste.

Beat 2 cups heavy cream until it begins to thicken (don't beat stiff). Add 2 tablespoons vinegar and 2 tablespoons lemon juice; carefully mix in with the vegetables. Mound the salad in a shallow bowl and sprinkle the top with 2 cups cooked ham, also cut julienne. If you want to splurge, garnish with a few slivers of truffles. Makes 8 generous servings.

Sausage Wilted Salad

If you like sausage, try this main-dish salad of fresh greens wilted with hot sausages and vinegar.

⅓ to ½ pound smoked sausages, cut in ½-inch pieces
  Small amount butter
⅓ cup cider vinegar
 2 tablespoons water
½ teaspoon salt
¼ teaspoon sugar
 1 head leaf lettuce, leaves torn in bite-sized pieces

Brown sausages in butter; pour off excess fat. Add vinegar, water, salt, and sugar. Heat to boiling. Pour sausages and liquid into a bowl over torn leaves of lettuce. Cover for a few seconds. Mix and serve. Makes 2 servings.

Cobb Salad

This interesting salad was created quite by accident over 30 years ago by Robert H. Cobb, then owner of the Little Hat Derby, forerunner of the Brown Derby restaurants in the Los Angeles area.

 1 large head iceberg lettuce
 1 bunch water cress
 3 hard-cooked eggs
12 slices crisp cooked bacon, crumbled (1 cup)
⅓ cup crumbled Roquefort or blue cheese
 4 medium-sized tomatoes, peeled
 2 medium-sized avocados
 2 boned cooked chicken breasts
 1 tablespoon chopped chives
   Butter lettuce
   Olives (optional)
   Radishes (optional)
   Avocado slices (optional)
   French dressing

Using the large blade of a food chopper or a French knife or cutting tool, coarsely chop the lettuce, water cress leaves (omit stems), hard-cooked eggs, bacon, cheese, tomatoes, avocados, chicken, and chives. Line plates with butter lettuce and pile salad on the plates, peaking it up. Garnish with olives, radishes, and avocado slices, if desired. Pass the dressing. Makes 4 servings.

Lorenzo Salad

For a satisfying salad luncheon, serve this refreshingly different version of the classic Lorenzo salad.

*1 head iceberg lettuce, cut in cubes, discarding
    the core
1 tomato, peeled and seeded
2 anchovy fillets, chopped
1 cooked whole chicken breast, diced
1 cup chopped water cress, stems discarded
⅓ cup olive oil
1½ tablespoons vinegar
¼ teaspoon salt
3 crushed whole black peppers
1 teaspoon chili sauce
1 hard-cooked egg, chopped
    Quartered tomatoes*

Mix the lettuce, peeled tomato, anchovy, chicken, and water cress. Dress with a mixture of olive oil, vinegar, salt, crushed whole black peppers, and chili sauce. Arrange salad in a mound in bowl; sprinkle top with chopped egg and garnish with quartered tomatoes. Makes 4 servings.

Hot Chicken Salad

Sesame seeds, mustard, coriander, and lemon juice flavor this hot chicken salad, which is an adaptation of a classic Chinese hot salad.

*2 tablespoons toasted sesame seed
2 tablespoons prepared mustard
2 tablespoons lemon juice
¼ cup chicken stock or water
½ teaspoon salt
½ teaspoon sugar
½ teaspoon ground coriander
½ cup chopped green onions
4 cups diced cooked chicken
    About 2 cups shredded iceberg lettuce*

In a pan, blend together the sesame seed, mustard, lemon juice, chicken stock or water, salt, sugar, coriander, and onions. Add the chicken and heat. Arrange the shredded lettuce on a warm platter and pour the hot chicken mixture over it. Serve immediately. Makes about 6 servings.

Pineapple Chicken Salad

The method of preparing this dish departs from the usual salad-making technique. The chicken and fruit cook together; a sauce is added, and all is then chilled.

*2 whole chicken breasts, boned, skinned, cut in
    small chunks
    Salt
3 tablespoons butter or margarine
1 tablespoon finely diced candied ginger
¼ cup finely chopped green onion (white part only)
2 cups fresh pineapple, cut in pieces about the same
    size as the chicken
⅓ cup sour cream
2 egg yolks
½ teaspoon powdered ginger
    Grated peel of 1 lemon
    Juice of 1 lemon
¼ cup chopped salted peanuts
    Pineapple shell (optional)
    Lettuce (optional)
    Chopped salted peanuts for garnish
    Thinly sliced rings of green onion tops for garnish*

Sprinkle chicken chunks with salt. Melt butter or margarine in a wide pan with candied ginger and chopped green onion. Add chicken and cook, stirring, over high heat just until meat turns white, 1 or 2 minutes. Remove meat from pan. Turn heat to high and add fresh pineapple; cook quickly, stirring, until fruit is lightly glazed. Reduce heat and return chicken to pan. Blend in the sour cream beaten with the egg yolks, powdered ginger, lemon peel, and lemon juice. Heat gently for 2 or 3 minutes, stirring. Do not boil. Cover and chill thoroughly, overnight perhaps. Just before serving, mix in the ¼ cup chopped salted peanuts. Serve in pineapple shell or lettuce-lined bowl. Garnish with additional chopped peanuts and thinly sliced rings of green onion tops. Makes 4 servings.

Chicken and Fruit Salad

This salad luncheon dish is distinguished in both appearance and flavor.

2½ to 3 cups diced, cooked chicken (cut in about
   ¾-inch cubes)
1 cup sliced celery
2 tablespoons chopped green onion
2 tablespoons capers
1 teaspoon salt
2 tablespoons lemon juice
1 can (11 oz.) mandarin oranges, drained
1 can (about 9 oz.) pineapple chunks or tidbits,
   drained
½ cup slivered almonds, toasted
½ cup mayonnaise
½ teaspoon grated lemon peel
   Salad greens

(Use leftover cooked chicken meat, or cook 2 whole chicken breasts in water to cover, seasoned with 1 teaspoon salt, 1 teaspoon monosodium glutamate, several whole black peppers, and 1 small onion, chopped; cook until tender, about 30 minutes. Cool.)

Combine the chicken with the celery, green onion, and capers. Mix in the salt and lemon juice; cover, and chill for several hours. Just before serving, add the oranges (reserve a few for garnish), pineapple, and almonds. Combine mayonnaise and lemon peel; mix in carefully so as not to break fruit. Spoon into a bowl lined with greens. Garnish with reserved oranges. Makes 6 servings.

Cold Chicken Salad Plates

For a spur-of-the-moment picnic, pick up a commercial barbecued chicken to serve with fresh and cooked vegetables in individual salad plates. If you prefer, you can broil game hens instead.

2 Rock Cornish game hens, split and broiled or 1
   barbecued broiler-fryer, quartered
4 yellow crookneck squash, sliced
1 package (9 oz.) frozen Italian green beans
   Boiling salted water
1 jar (6 oz.) marinated artichoke hearts
2 tablespoons lemon juice
¼ teaspoon salt
¼ teaspoon garlic salt
½ teaspoon mixed salad herbs or mixed thyme,
   basil, and tarragon
12 cherry tomatoes
1 small cucumber

Chill the cooked halved game hens or quartered chicken. Separately cook the squash and green beans in boiling salted water until barely tender, about 5 to 7 minutes for each, and drain well; cool.

For the dressing, pour off marinade from the artichoke hearts and blend in lemon juice, salt, garlic salt, and crushed herbs.

Select four baking dishes, foil pans, or ramekins, about 7 or 8 inches in diameter. Arrange in each one a chicken piece and a spoonful of green beans and squash. Garnish with cherry tomatoes and sliced cucumber. Spoon dressing over the vegetables and chill before serving. Makes 4 servings.

Asparagus and Shrimp Platter

This chilled salad comes from Sweden where it is sometimes served as part of a smörgåsbord.

21 to 24 shrimp (40-to-the-pound size)
*   *Boiling salted water*
14 to 16 very large, fat asparagus spears, all trimmed
*   *about 4 inches long*
⅓ cup salad oil
⅓ cup lemon juice
¼ teaspoon dill weed
¼ teaspoon dry mustard
½ teaspoon salt
*   *Lemon wedges*
*   *Parsley sprigs*

Devein shrimp by inserting a slender wooden or metal skewer into the back in several places and gently pulling up through the back to draw out the vein. Cook in boiling salted water to cover until shrimp turn pink; drain and shell the shrimp when they are cool enough to touch.

Lay asparagus spears flat and parallel in a wide pan, in just enough boiling salted water to cover. Cook until asparagus is tender when pierced with tip of a sharp knife; drain. In a wide, rimmed dish, arrange the asparagus spears on one side (keeping spears parallel) and the shrimp alongside. Mix together salad oil, lemon juice, dill weed, dry mustard and salt, and pour over shellfish and vegetables. Cover and chill.

To serve, arrange asparagus on a large round platter, tips pointed to the center in a pinwheel. Loop 2 shrimp over every other spear, 1 shrimp over each of the remaining spears. (In Sweden whole boiled crayfish are used instead of the shrimp; you might make this substitution if and when you can get this fresh-water shellfish.) Allow at least 2 spears for each serving. Garnish with lemon and parsley. Makes 7 to 8 servings.

Shrimp and Citrus Salad Bowl

This eye-catching fruit and seafood salad is most effective to mix at the table before your guests. You may assemble it several hours in advance and chill it until you are ready to serve.

Plump asparagus spears are looped with pink shrimp in Asparagus and Shrimp Platter salad.

1 head romaine lettuce
1 head endive or 2 heads iceberg lettuce
1 pound cooked small ocean shrimp or 3 cans
*   (5 oz. each) shrimp*
2 oranges
1 grapefruit
1 can (14 oz.) hearts of palm
*   Water cress for garnish*

DRESSING:

⅓ cup olive oil
2 tablespoons wine vinegar
¼ teaspoon salt
¼ teaspoon dry mustard
⅓ cup cocktail sauce or chili sauce

Line the bottom and sides of a large shallow salad bowl with romaine and tear remaining romaine and endive into bite-sized pieces and lay inside the bowl. Mound the shrimp in the center. Cut rind and all white membrane off oranges, then slice them. Cut off grapefruit rind the same way; lift out the segments. Surround shrimp with orange slices and grapefruit segments. Drain hearts of palm and slice into ½-inch pieces. Garnish with water cress. Chill until ready to serve.

To make Chili Dressing, shake together the olive oil, wine vinegar, salt, mustard, and cocktail sauce until well blended. At the table, pour dressing over salad mix, and serve. Makes 6 servings.

Summer Shrimp Salad

A San Francisco hotel chef who has spent much of his career on the Riviera serves this variation of Salade Nicoise. The salad is pictured on the cover of this book.

To make the salad, follow the directions for Salade Nicoise on page 22, omitting the anchovy fillets, capers, tuna, and water cress. Use 1 tomato and 1 or 2 hard-cooked eggs. Line a round shallow platter with butter lettuce. Place the marinated potato slices down the center and spoon the marinated green beans on each side. Peel tomato and cut in wedges; arrange on green beans on only one side of platter. Peel and quarter eggs and arrange on the beans on the other side. Place a row of 6 to 8 ripe olives down the center of the potatoes, alternating with a rolled anchovy fillet stuffed with caper. Flank olives with ⅓ pound

Summer Shrimp Salad is a variation of Salade Niçoise, on page 22. Serve with French bread and butter.

peeled and cooked medium shrimp. Sprinkle with chopped chives. Spoon additional vinaigrette dressing on salad just before serving. Makes 3 or 4 servings.

Prawn Salad with Green Goddess Dressing

Begin preparations for this salad the night before by cooking the prawns and cutting the celery. Mix with dressing just before serving.

2 pounds uncooked prawns or large shrimp
1 quart celery pieces
  Green Goddess Dressing (recipe follows)
  Iceberg lettuce
  Parsley

The night before, shell and devein prawns. Put prawns in a large saucepan, cover with water and bring to a boil. Remove immediately from heat. Allow to cool for 15 minutes. Rinse in cold water and cut each prawn in half, lengthwise (save a few whole ones for garnish). Pick whitest stalks of celery; clean thoroughly. Cut in ⅛-inch-thick slices; combine with prawns and refrigerate overnight. Dress with Green Goddess Dressing to barely coat (about 1 cup). Pile lightly into a shallow salad bowl lined with large leaves of iceberg lettuce. Garnish with whole prawns and parsley sprigs; serve dressing on the side. Makes 16 servings.

GREEN GODDESS DRESSING:

  2 cups mayonnaise
  1 cup white wine vinegar
  1 small can (2 oz.) rolled anchovies with capers
½ cup chopped fresh parsley
  1 small onion, finely chopped (about ½ cup)
  2 teaspoons dried tarragon leaves
½ teaspoon salt
  1 cup whipping cream

Place mayonnaise, ¾ cup of the vinegar, drained anchovies, parsley, onion, tarragon, and salt into blender; whirl until thoroughly blended. Combine remaining vinegar with cream and add to first mixture. Whirl again. Store in refrigerator until needed. Makes 4 cups dressing.

Mushrooms, crab, Belgian endive, and avocado go together in delectable Treasure Island Salad.

Treasure Island Salad

For the occasion of the 1939 Golden Gate International Exposition, a famous San Francisco hotel chef created this fine crab and avocado combination salad; hence its name, Treasure Island. Since then, it has been practically forgotten, but recently was rediscovered.

½ *pound fresh mushrooms, washed and thinly sliced*
2 *cups thinly sliced celery*
1 *can (2 oz.) sliced pimiento*
½ *cup olive oil*
¼ *cup white wine vinegar*
½ *teaspoon salt*
½ *teaspoon dry mustard*
  Freshly ground pepper to taste
  Romaine
1 *pound crab legs*
4 *bunches Belgian endive*
1 *avocado*
1 *lemon, cut in wedges*

Mix mushroom slices together lightly with the celery and pimiento. For the dressing, shake together the oil, vinegar, salt, mustard, and pepper to taste; pour enough of the dressing over the mushroom mixture just to coat it lightly. Cover and chill.

Line four plates with romaine and spoon mushroom mixture into one section at top of plates. Place crab legs at the base. Separate Belgian endive into leaves; fan out the endive from one side of crab legs. Cut avocado in half, peel, and slice. Arrange slices fanning out from crab opposite the endive. Arrange lemon wedges on the plates. Spoon over remaining dressing. Makes 4 servings.

Aloha Crab Salad Platter

Hawaiian fruits enhance the delicacy of crab in this handsome, serve-yourself salad platter. A spicy Polynesian dressing and macadamia nuts complement the flavors of the four fruits and seafood.

1 *small pineapple*
1 *avocado*
  Juice of 1 lemon
1 *papaya*
2 *cans (11 oz. each) mandarin oranges*
  Greens (optional)
1 *pound Alaska king crab meat*
½ *pint (1 cup) sour cream*
  Juice and grated peel of 1 lime
⅓ *cup finely chopped chutney*
1 *cup macadamia nuts, chopped*

Peel pineapple, removing eyes carefully, and slice into ½-inch-thick rounds; then cut out the core and cut each slice in half. Halve, peel, and slice the avocado, and dip the slices into lemon juice. Peel papaya, halve, and remove seeds, then slice. Drain mandarin oranges. Select a large rectangular tray about 12 by 18 inches; line it with greens, if you wish. Arrange on it rows of pineapple half slices, avocado slices, crab meat, papaya slices, and mandarin oranges. Cover the tray with clear plastic film and then chill it until serving time.

Mix the sour cream with the juice and grated peel of the lime and the chopped chutney. Turn into a small bowl and chill. Spoon macadamia nuts into a matching small bowl. At serving time, offer

Hawaiian fruits and Alaska king crab create decorative salad platter to serve buffet style. Offer small bowls of chutney-spiked sour cream dressing and chopped macadamia nuts to spoon over servings.

the fruit and crab tray, and pass the sour cream-chutney dressing and chopped nut meats to spoon over the individual servings. Makes 6 servings.

Papaya and Crab Salad

For a guest luncheon, fill half-shells of papaya with crab meat and serve with special Russian Dressing.

Peel 3 papayas, halve, and scoop out seeds. Arrange on greens on 6 individual plates. Fill papayas with 1½ pounds Dungeness or king crab meat. Garnish plates with marinated artichoke hearts and pitted olives. Serve with Russian Dressing (recipe follows).

DRESSING:

Blend together ½ cup mayonnaise, ½ cup sour cream, 3 tablespoons chili sauce, 3 tablespoons lime juice, ¼ teaspoon salt, and 1 teaspoon sugar. Mix in 3 tablespoons chopped chives. Pass to spoon over each salad. Makes 6 servings.

Crab Salad Oriental

Serve peeled tomato wedges with this crab salad. You can have it ready and waiting long before guests are due.

2 cans (1 lb. each) bean sprouts, drained
2 cups lightly packed chopped water cress leaves
2 tablespoons olive oil or salad oil
3 tablespoons lime juice
1½ teaspoons salt
2 cans (7½ oz. each) king crab meat, drained
1½ to 2 cups mayonnaise, freshly made or
    commercial
2 tablespoons drained capers
Water cress or lettuce leaves

Mix bean sprouts and chopped water cress with oil, lime juice, and salt. Mound slightly on a serving platter. Reserve a few whole pieces of crab; place remainder on vegetable mixture. Spread the whole with the mayonnaise. Decorate with capers and reserved crab. Arrange water cress or lettuce around the salad. Cover lightly and chill for 1 to 2 hours. Makes 6 servings.

Meat, Fish, Poultry Salads   49

Crab and Apple Salad

The ingredients in this salad will remind you of Waldorf salad, but the crab makes the effect refreshingly different.

1½ cups chopped celery
  2 cups cooked, fresh, frozen, or canned crab meat
    in large pieces
½ cup chopped walnuts
  1 Winesap apple, cored, and cut in slivers (about
    1 cup)
½ cup mayonnaise
    Salt
    Lettuce leaves
    Red apple slices
    Lemon wedges (optional)

Lightly mix together the celery, crab, walnuts, slivered apple, mayonnaise, and salt to taste. (If you make the salad ahead, cover and chill for several hours.) Mound salad onto lettuce in a bowl or on individual dishes. Garnish with apple slices and lemon wedges, to squeeze over salad if desired, Makes 6 first course or 4 main-dish servings.

Luncheon salad of fresh crab is dressed with crab butter blended with olive oil and lemon juice.

Fresh Crab Salad

Crab "butter," the flavorful, soft substance you find inside the shell when you crack crab, is used in the dressing for this salad. Crab butter is cream-colored in a live crab, but turns yellow when the crab is boiled.

Boil, clean, and crack live crabs, saving the yellow crab butter as you remove the meat from the shell. Chill the crab meat and crab butter until you are ready to make the salads.

For each crab, blend crab butter with 1 tablespoon olive oil or salad oil, 1½ tablespoons lemon juice, 1 tablespoon chopped parsley, and 1 green onion (including part of the top), chopped. Mix dressing with crab meat and serve on shredded lettuce. Garnish with tomato wedges, slices of hard-cooked egg, ripe olives, and lemon wedges. A medium-sized crab serves 1 generously as a main course, 3 or 4 as a first course.

Crab Louis

Which Louis originated this hearty, full-meal salad, we do not know, but Solari's Grill in San Francisco was among the first restaurants to serve it, around 1911. Now it is a favorite in many restaurants. Louis dressing is also good on shrimp.

1 cup mayonnaise
¼ cup whipping cream
¼ cup chili sauce
¼ cup chopped green pepper
¼ cup chopped green onion
    Salt to taste
    Lemon juice to taste
2 heads iceberg lettuce
2 large Dungeness crabs, cracked and shelled, or
    1½ to 2 pounds crab meat
4 large tomatoes
4 hard-cooked eggs

Mix together the mayonnaise, whipping cream, chili sauce, green pepper, and green onion. Season with salt and lemon juice to taste. Arrange outer leaves of lettuce on 4 large plates; shred the heart of the lettuce and arrange a bed of shredded lettuce in the center of the leaves. Place the body meat of

Crab Chalupas Compuestas is fascinating hot and cold salad of tortilla, refried beans, crab, avocado.

the crabs on the shredded lettuce. Cut tomatoes and eggs in sixths and arrange symmetrically around the crab. Pour over the Louis dressing, and garnish with crab legs. Makes 4 servings.

Shellfish Artichoke Salad

This salad is based on the Fresh Herb Mayonnaise Salad on page 52. The fresh mayonnaise, which you can make before your guests, is blended only with shellfish for this salad and served from cooked, marinated artichoke cases.

To make the salad, follow the directions in Fresh Herb Mayonnaise Salad, increasing the amount of crab to 2 cups and the amount of large and small shrimp to 4 cups, leaving out the lettuces and spinach. Serve the salad in cooked artichoke cases prepared in this manner: Break small course outer bracts from 6 to 8 large artichokes; trim top third from each artichoke and cut off remaining

thorny tips with scissors. Cook in boiling salted water until tender. Drain, coat with an oil and vinegar dressing, and chill. Drain, open out artichoke bracts, scoop out fuzzy centers, and fill with the shellfish mixture. Makes 6 to 8 luncheon main-dish servings.

Crab Chalupas Compuestas

One Mexican restaurant in San Francisco makes a specialty of this hot salad version of the popular tostada. It is served in a low, round basket. On a bed of shredded greens, built up in layers, are crisp tortilla, hot refried beans, shredded Cheddar cheese, crab meat, and seasoned avocado. A surprising combination, perhaps, but it is delicious. Occasionally, you may want to substitute sliced chicken, turkey, or shrimp for the crab meat.

¼ cup salad oil
4 tortillas
1 avocado
2 tablespoons lime juice
¼ teaspoon garlic salt
1 large head iceberg lettuce
1 can (1 lb., 4 oz.) refried beans
1 cup shredded mild Cheddar cheese
¾ to 1 pound Alaska king crab meat
2 medium-sized tomatoes
½ cup pitted ripe olives
  Prepared tacos sauce

Heat oil in a large frying pan; add tortillas, one at a time, and let heat until crisp and brown, about 2 minutes on each side. Halve avocado, peel, and remove seed. Mash the fruit and blend in the lime juice and garlic salt.

Line four plates with the outer lettuce leaves, then finely shred the inside head and mound on the plates. Heat the beans until they start to bubble. Arrange a crisp tortilla on top of the greens on each plate, and spoon over the hot refried beans. Sprinkle with cheese, and cover with a layer of crab meat (save some for garnish). Spoon on avocado mixture; garnish with crab pieces. Surround with sliced tomato and ripe olives. Pass a pitcher of prepared tacos sauce. Makes 4 servings.

Stuffed Tomato Salad

Here is a rather dressy, but easy-to-make platter salad. Tomatoes are filled with crab meat and artichokes and garnished with avocado and egg. A rich dressing is served with the salad.

6 medium-sized tomatoes, peeled
1 cup fresh crab legs (or 1 can, 7½-oz. size, crab meat)
1 jar (6 oz.) marinated artichoke hearts, drained
Shredded lettuce
1 avocado, peeled and sliced
3 hard-cooked eggs, cut in wedges
Pitted ripe olives or stuffed Spanish-style green olives

DRESSING:

1 cup mayonnaise
¼ cup heavy cream
¼ cup chili sauce
1 tablespoon lemon juice

Remove cores from tomatoes and turn smooth side (bottom) up. Cut each tomato almost all the way through to make a wheel of 6 or 8 evenly spaced wedges. Fill between wedges, alternately, with small portions of crab and artichoke. Place tomatoes on a tray covered with the shredded lettuce. Garnish with avocado, egg, and olives.

Blend mayonnaise with cream, chili sauce, and lemon juice, and pour into a small bowl. Spoon dressing generously. Makes 6 servings.

Fresh Herb Mayonnaise Salad

You can make the mayonnaise for this salad before your guests in two minutes or less! Then you mix the salad and serve. Two pieces of equipment are indispensable: a large salad bowl and a wire whip. It's more fun if the bowl is clear enough to see through, but crockery, enameled metal, or wood can be used.

½ teaspoon dry mustard
About 1 teaspoon salt
2 tablespoons minced parsley
1 tablespoon minced chives (fresh, frozen or freeze-dried)
2 teaspoons crumbled tarragon
Juice of 1 lemon
1 egg
¾ cup salad oil
½ cup sour cream
1 cup fresh or frozen crab meat
2 to 3 cups cooked shrimp (a combination of large shrimp, split lengthwise, and small whole shrimp)
1 large head iceberg lettuce, broken in bite-sized pieces (about 5 cups)
1 large head butter lettuce, broken in bite-sized pieces (about 5 cups)
2 to 3 cups tender spinach leaves, broken in bite-sized pieces

Put the mustard in the salad bowl along with 1 teaspoon of the salt, parsley, chives, and tarragon. Soften the lemon by rolling it under your hand on a flat surface.

On a tray group the lemon and a small knife (or cut the lemon in half in the kitchen), the egg, a small pitcher containing the oil, a dish with the sour cream, the shellfish in a bowl, and the lettuces and spinach in a bowl or wire basket. You will also need a wire whisk and salad mixers. Bring this tray and the salad bowl to the table, buffet, cart, or small table in the dining area before your guests.

Slice the lemon in half and squeeze the juice from both portions into the bowl. Break the egg into the bowl. Blend ingredients in the bowl with the wire whip, then slowly add about 1 tablespoon of oil at a time, beating constantly, for a total of five additions. The mixture should look opaque. Then pour in remaining oil in a slow stream,

beating continually until all oil is used.

Stir sour cream into mayonnaise, then add the crab and shrimp, mixing to coat with dressing. Add the greens and lightly toss until leaves are well coated. Season with more salt if needed and serve immediately. Makes 8 to 10 servings.

Combination Slaw with Sardines

Cole slaw takes on new interest with the addition of sardines and bacon. This salad is made with a cooked dressing.

   2 slices bacon, diced
   2 tablespoons minced onion
   1 tablespoon flour
   1 teaspoon dry mustard
   2 tablespoons vinegar
   ½ cup water
   2½ cups shredded red cabbage
   2½ cups shredded green cabbage
   ½ cup diced green pepper
   2 cans (3¼ oz. each) sardines, drained
      Salt and pepper
      Lemon slices

Fry bacon until crisp; remove pieces and reserve. Add onion to the bacon fat and cook slowly 1 minute. Remove from heat; stir in the flour and mustard; add vinegar and water and mix thoroughly. Cook, stirring, until thickened; cool.

Mix in a bowl the cabbage, green pepper, bacon, and 1 can of the sardines, chopped. Pour the dressing over top and mix; adjust seasoning if needed. Garnish with the sardines from remaining can and lemon slices. Makes 4 to 6 servings.

Abalone Salad

This salad contains chunks of richly flavored canned abalone mixed with red and green vegetables and mounded in crisp lettuce cups. It makes an unusual first course for a company meal.

   1 can (5¼ oz.) cubed abalone
   1 cup thinly sliced celery
   ¼ cup chopped green onions, including some of the tops
   6 radishes, thinly sliced crosswise
   ½ cup diced green pepper
   ¼ cup chopped pimiento
   7 or 8 green olives, chopped
      Mayonnaise (about ½ cup)
   6 lettuce cups
      Hard-cooked eggs, sliced

Mix together abalone cubes, celery, green onion, radishes, green pepper, pimiento, and green olives with mayonnaise to moisten. Arrange lettuce cups on a chop plate, or in individual serving dishes; fill with abalone salad. Garnish with hard-cooked egg slices. Makes 6 servings.

Sardine Salad

The onions and celery in this hearty salad mellow the decisive flavor of the sardines and add desirable crispness. Chives may be substituted for the onions.

   1 can (4½ oz.) sardines
   1 hard-cooked egg
   ¼ cup finely chopped green onions, tops and all
   ½ cup finely sliced celery
   1 cup chilled cooked peas
      Mayonnaise
      Lettuce
      Paprika, sliced stuffed olives, lemon wedges

Chop sardines and hard-cooked egg together. Stir in green onions, celery, and peas. Mix with enough mayonnaise to hold together. Chill. Serve in mounds on lettuce. Sprinkle with paprika. Garnish with stuffed olives and serve with lemon wedges and mayonnaise. Makes 4 to 6 servings.

Salmon Fruit Salad

Be sure to use firm-ripe bananas in this salad; if too soft, they will become mushy.

1½ cups cold salmon (cooked or canned), boned and
    in chunks
½ cup fresh or canned pineapple chunks
1 cup coarsely diced firm-ripe banana
¾ cup chopped celery
¼ cup firmly chopped dill pickle
2 tablespoons mayonnaise
1 tablespoon Dijon-style prepared mustard
    Salt
    Lettuce leaves
    Lemon wedges (optional)

Combine salmon, pineapple, banana, celery, and dill pickle in a bowl. Blend mayonnaise and mustard, and mix lightly with the salmon mixture. Salt as needed. (You can cover and chill salad for an hour or two if you want to make it ahead.)

Mound salad onto lettuce leaves arranged on individual dishes or in a bowl. Serve with lemon wedges to squeeze over salad if desired. Makes 5 first course or 3 main-dish servings.

Swedish Salmon Plate

For a spur-of-the-moment guest dinner, you can use several convenience foods for this instant main-dish salad. It can also be prepared in advance and chilled, ready to serve luncheon guests.

1 can (1 lb.) salmon, drained
½ pound asparagus, cooked and chilled
⅓ pound mushrooms, sliced
⅓ cup olive oil or salad oil
2½ tablespoons white wine vinegar
¼ teaspoon salt
¼ teaspoon dry mustard
    Greens
1 cucumber, sliced thinly
2 tomatoes, cut in wedges
    Sour Cream Dressing (recipe follows)

Remove bones from salmon, leaving fish in large fillets. Place the fish, asparagus, and mushrooms separately in a shallow dish. Mix together the oil, vinegar, salt, and mustard and spoon over; cover and chill 1 hour. Arrange greens on an oval platter, place fish fillets in the center, and radiate spokes of asparagus from the fish. Place mushrooms at either end. Arrange cucumber slices on the sides, flanked by tomato wedges. Accompany with Sour Cream Dressing (recipe follows). Makes 6 servings.

SOUR CREAM DRESSING:

Mix together ½ cup mayonnaise, ½ cup sour cream, 1 tablespoon anchovy paste, 2 tablespoons chopped parsley, 2 tablespoons capers, and salt and pepper to taste. Makes 1¼ cups.

Oyster Salad

A generous portion of this salad makes an ideal main dish for a luncheon; or serve it to accompany baked ham or tongue at a guest buffet.

1 cup tarragon vinegar
3 cups water
1 teaspoon salt
1 teaspoon tarragon
2 pints oysters
1 cup mayonnaise
1 teaspoon lemon juice
1 tablespoon anchovy paste
1 teaspoon grated onion
    Salt and white pepper to taste
1 large bunch celery, sliced very fine
    Anchovy fillets and stuffed green olives

Combine tarragon vinegar with water, salt, and tarragon. Bring to a boil. Add oysters and cook for about 2 minutes, or just until the oysters plump and begin to curl on the edges. Drain oysters and chill thoroughly. Mix mayonnaise with lemon juice, anchovy paste, and onion. To serve, mix half of mayonnaise mixture with the oysters; season with salt and pepper. Make a bed of sliced celery on a platter or individual plates. Mound oysters on top; top with remaining mayonnaise mixture and garnish with anchovy fillets and olives. Makes 4 main-dish servings or about 8 smaller servings.

Pickled Tuna Salad

The tangy dressing on this tuna salad is a refreshing change from mayonnaise dressing.

1 can (6½ oz.) chunk tuna, drained
½ cup white wine vinegar (or use ⅓ cup to decrease
*   the pickled flavor)*
½ medium-sized onion, chopped
¼ teaspoon dill seed
1 bay leaf
*   Dash allspice*
¼ teaspoon dry mustard
½ cup sliced celery
¼ cup mayonnaise
6 tomato slices (optional)
6 lettuce leaves

In a bowl, break tuna into pieces with a fork. In a small saucepan, combine vinegar, onion, dill seed, bay leaf, allspice, and mustard; bring to a boil. Pour over tuna; refrigerate several hours or overnight. Just before serving, drain tuna thoroughly; combine with celery and mayonnaise. Make 6 individual salads by spooning tuna mixture onto a tomato slice on a lettuce leaf (or omit the tomato slice and just use lettuce). Makes 6 servings.

Tuna Salad, Oriental

Some rather unlikely flavors and textures combine to make this salad that's nearly a full meal.

4 cans (7 oz. each) tuna, drained
2 cans (5 oz. each) water chestnuts, drained and
*   sliced*
1 can (1 lb.) bean sprouts, drained
1 can (1 lb.) pitted ripe olives, drained
2 cups seedless green grapes
¼ cup chopped dill pickle
1 large or 2 small avocados
½ cup sour cream
½ cup prepared sandwich spread
¼ teaspoon seasoned salt
¼ teaspoon garlic salt
*   Crisp salad greens*
*   Tomato wedges*

Break tuna in bite-sized chunks into a large bowl. Add sliced water chestnuts, bean sprouts, whole olives, grapes, and pickle. Peel and slice avocado, and add to salad. Mix gently. Chill thoroughly.

Meanwhile, make dressing by combining the sour cream, sandwich spread, seasoned salt, and garlic salt. To serve, add dressing to salad and turn out on a large platter lined with greens. Garnish with tomato wedges. Makes 6 to 8 servings.

Smoked Fish Salad with Chervil Dressing

Flaked fish is used to stuff these attractive tomato salads; chervil-flavored dressing is spooned on top.

1 pound smoked salmon or cod
8 medium-sized tomatoes
2 cups mayonnaise
2 teaspoons chevil (or use dill weed or finely
*   chopped fresh parsley)*
*   Dash of Worcestershire*
*   Salt and pepper to taste*
*   Lettuce*

Set the piece of fish on a rack over boiling water in a steamer; steam just until heated through, about 10 to 15 minutes. Cool, remove bones, and flake. Cut tops from the tomatoes; remove the pulp with a spoon, saving the pulp and discarding the tomato seeds. Fill each of the tomato cups with the flaked fish. For the dressing, chop and combine the tomato pulp with mayonnaise, chervil, Worcestershire, salt and pepper to taste. Spoon part of dressing on top each tomato cup; pass additional dressing at the table. Serve each tomato cup on a crisp lettuce leaf. Makes 8 servings.

Egg, Cheese, Rice, & Paste Salads

CREAMY, RICH, AND FILLING

The salads in this chapter lend themselves as main dishes or as accompaniments. They make especially good choices for barbecue menus since most of them can be prepared well in advance; many actually improve when chilled for a while, giving flavors a chance to blend. Paste salads also stand up well if they have to wait a bit while the entrée is being served.

Most of the salads in this group are hearty. Use them to replace an oven-baked casserole accompaniment for a main dish, and you might even serve them in lettuce-lined casseroles as an interesting change from the usual salad bowl.

Feature one of these rich creamy salads in your next picnic menu, for they are perfect replacements for the old standby, potato salad. Try them, too, for warm-weather meals, with sliced cold meats, a fresh-baked hot bread, and a refreshing beverage. And don't overlook these salads when planning the main dish for a party luncheon.

Garnishes are important here, for often egg, cheese, rice, and paste salads are not colorful in themselves. A wedge of bright red tomato, a sprig of deep green water cress, or a ring of golden pineapple will add a touch of color as well as a flavor note of its own.

Hollowed beefsteak tomato half holds enough crab and rice salad for main-dish serving. Recipe for Crab-Rice Salad Bowl on page 60.

Swiss Cheese Salad

This classic Swiss cheese salad is best served as an accompaniment for roast or barbecued beef.

1 pound natural Swiss cheese cut in ¼-inch cubes
3 hard-cooked eggs, diced (reserve 1 yolk for garnish)
½ cup chopped celery
½ cup chopped green pepper
½ cup mayonnaise
1 tablespoon chopped chives
2 teaspoons white wine vinegar
1½ teaspoons prepared mustard
¼ teaspoon salt
Lettuce leaves
Cherry tomatoes for garnish

Mix together the cheese, eggs, celery, and green pepper. In another bowl, blend together the mayonnaise, chives, vinegar, mustard, and salt. Stir the dressing into the cheese mixture and refrigerate the salad until serving time.

To serve, mound the salad on individual lettuce leaves or in a bowl lined with lettuce.

Press the reserved egg yolk through a fine wire strainer and sprinkle over the salad. Use cherry tomatoes to garnish. (They add color, and the tomato-cheese flavor combination is delicious.) Makes 6 servings.

Swiss Cheese-Potato Salad

For this cheese-potato salad, you have a choice of dressings: a tart French dressing flavored with basil, or a creamy mayonnaise dressing with horse-radish. You might arrange this entrée salad on a large platter and surround it with cold sliced meats and tomato wedges.

  1 pound natural Swiss cheese, cut in ¼-inch cubes
  4 cups cooked, peeled, diced potatoes
  3 hard-cooked eggs, diced
  ½ cup chopped celery
  ½ cup chopped green onions
  ½ cup sliced radishes
  ¼ cup chopped green pepper
    Basil French Dressing or
      Horse-radish Mayonnaise Dressing
  2 tablespoons chopped parsley for garnish

  Mix together the cheese, potatoes, eggs, celery, onions, radishes, and green pepper. Blend in one of the dressings given below and refrigerate. To serve, garnish with the chopped parsley. Makes 6 to 8 servings.

BASIL FRENCH DRESSING:

  Blend together ⅔ cup salad oil, ⅓ cup basil white wine vinegar, 1 tablespoon lemon juice, 1 mashed clove garlic, ¾ teaspoon salt, ½ teaspoon basil, and a dash of pepper.

HORSE-RADISH MAYONNAISE DRESSING:

  Blend together 1 cup mayonnaise, 1 tablespoon prepared horse-radish (or to taste), and ½ teaspoon salt.

Western Cheese Salad

This crab and cheese salad is a good luncheon entrée. Mound individual servings on lettuce leaves and serve with a cold relish tray.

  1 pound Swiss cheese, cut in ¼-inch cubes
  1 cup cooked crab meat
  ½ cup chopped celery
  ¼ cup chopped green pepper
  ½ cup sour cream
  1½ tablespoons lemon juice
  2 teaspoons chopped chives
  ½ teaspoon dill weed
  ¼ teaspoon salt
  ¼ teaspoon sugar
    Dash pepper
    Lettuce leaves
    Tomato wedges and parsley for garnish

  Mix together the cheese, crab, celery, and green pepper. In another bowl, blend the sour cream, lemon juice, chives, dill weed, salt, sugar, and pepper. Combine the dressing with the cheese mixture and refrigerate. To serve, mound on individual lettuce leaves; garnish with tomato wedges and parsley. Makes 6 servings.

Onion and Cheese Salad

Julienne pieces of Swiss cheese, ham, and green pepper are combined with sweet onion rings for this salad.

  1 large sweet onion, sliced very thinly
  ¼ pound Swiss cheese, cut julienne
  ¼ pound cooked ham, cut julienne
  1 large green pepper, cut julienne
  3 tablespoons wine vinegar
  ⅓ cup salad oil (part olive oil, if desired)
    Salt and freshly ground pepper to taste
    Lettuce

  Cut onion slices in half, separate rings, and cover with ice water. Chill for about 2 hours. Combine julienne pieces of Swiss cheese, ham, and green pepper with drained onion. Stir in vinegar, salad oil, salt, and pepper. Chill. Serve on lettuce. Makes 6 servings.

Double Cheese Salad

Crumbled, crisp bacon—a whole cup of it— turns cottage cheese and Roquefort into a hearty salad with a decisive flavor.

  2 cups (1 pound) creamed cottage cheese
½ cup crumbled Roquefort or blue cheese
  1 cup crumbled crisp bacon (½ pound)
  2 tablespoons sliced stuffed olives
  2 tablespoons mayonnaise
    Lettuce or chicory

Blend the cottage cheese with the Roquefort or blue cheese, crisp bacon, olives, and mayonnaise; chill for 1 hour. Serve on crisp lettuce or chicory. Makes 6 servings.

Rice Pilaf Salad

Cook the rice for this salad in time to chill it before adding the dressing.

Add ½ cup quick cooking brown rice to ¾ cup boiling water with 1 cube chicken bouillon. Reduce heat and steam for 15 minutes. Chill. Make dressing by combining 3 tablespoons mayonnaise, 3 tablespoons chopped canned mushrooms, 2 tablespoons lemon juice, ¼ teaspoon thyme, and ¼ teaspoon curry. Mix with chilled rice and arrange on lettuce-lined salad plates. Makes 2 servings.

Western Patio Salad

A fluffy hot dressing converts macaroni into this rich salad.

½ cup vinegar
½ cup water
½ cup sugar
  1 teaspoon dry mustard
  2 tablespoons flour
¼ teaspoon paprika
¼ teaspoon celery salt
¼ teaspoon salt
  2 eggs, separated, yolks and whites beaten separately
  1 tablespoon butter or margarine
½ cup light cream
  2 cups uncooked salad macaroni
    Boiling salted water
    Pimiento or quartered tomatoes for garnish

Bring vinegar and water to boiling point. Mix the sugar, mustard, flour, paprika, celery salt, salt, and beaten egg yolks together and stir into vinegar and water. Cook until thick. Remove from heat, add butter, and fold in stiffly beaten egg whites and cream. Cook macaroni as usual in plenty of boiling salted water; drain, blanch, and mix with hot dressing. Chill salad and serve with a garnish of pimiento or quartered tomatoes. Makes 6 servings.

Poached Egg Salad

This salad idea may be startling, but it's a very good way to begin a luncheon, or to add an unusual dish to a smörgåsbord buffet.

Poach as many eggs as there are persons to be served. When done to your liking, lift carefully and place in cold water.

Peel tomatoes carefully and cut in slices 1 inch thick (this sometimes takes the whole tomato). Arrange each tomato slice on a nest of lettuce; sprinkle with salt, pepper, and a little chopped basil. Put well drained, trimmed egg on top. For 6 eggs, mix 1 cup mayonnaise with ¼ cup chili sauce, ½ teaspoon minced basil, 2 teaspoons minced chives, and 2 teaspoons minced parsley. Pour over eggs and serve with crisp cheese sticks.

Stuffed Pimiento Salad

Bright red pimientos hold this fruit-flavored macaroni salad, which is good with cold slices of turkey or fried chicken.

  2 cups cooked mararoni
½ cup crushed pineapple, drained
  1 medium-sized tomato, diced
½ teaspoon salt
    Dash of pepper
  2 teaspoons prepared mustard
  3 tablespoons sour cream
  4 teaspoons wine vinegar
  1 teaspoon scraped onion
  2 jars or cans (4 oz. each) whole pimientos
    Lettuce
    Green onions (optional)

Combine the cooked macaroni with the drained pineapple, tomato, salt, and pepper. Mix together the mustard, sour cream, wine vinegar, and onion. Mix this dressing with the macaroni mixture. Drain the whole pimientos and stuff each with the macaroni salad. Serve on a bed of lettuce; surround with green onions if you wish. Makes 4 to 6 servings.

Crab-Rice Salad Bowl

Select large, firm, fairly smooth tomatoes to use as shells for this main dish salad.

  3 large beefsteak tomatoes
  2 cups frozen crab meat or 2 cans (7½ oz. each)
        crab meat, flaked
  1 cup cooked rice
  1 can (4 oz.) water chestnuts, drained and sliced
⅓ cup slivered almonds
⅓ cup chopped green pepper
½ cup mayonnaise
¼ cup tarragon vinegar
½ teaspoon oregano
  1 teaspoon salt
    Lettuce
    Green pepper rings, sliced hard-cooked egg,
      parsley for garnish

To make bowls, slice tomatoes in half horizontally; with a spoon hollow out the inside, saving pulp. Invert tomato halves on paper towel to drain. Discard seeds and dice the pulp.

In a bowl, mix together crab meat, rice, water chestnuts, almonds, green pepper, and tomato pulp. Combine mayonnaise, vinegar, oregano, and salt; fold into crab mixture. Lightly salt the inside of each tomato half and place on a bed of lettuce on individual serving plates. Fill with crab salad; garnish each salad with green pepper, hard-cooked egg, and parsley. Makes 6 servings.

Cracked Wheat Salad

Mix together 2 cups cooked cracked wheat or bulgur with ½ cup Italian style dressing. Chill at least 30 minutes. Mix with about 1 quart bite-sized pieces iceberg lettuce. Season to taste with salt and freshly ground pepper. Makes 6 servings.

Lunch on a tray offers Egg-Cottage Cheese Salad, avocado wedges, and hot English muffins.

Egg-Cottage Cheese Salad

When assembled on a large tray along with toasted English muffins, this cottage cheese salad makes a complete lunch. Prepare the salad an hour or more before time to serve; unmold it on the serving tray and chill in the refrigerator.

 6 hard-cooked eggs, peeled
 1 pint cottage cheese
 ½ to ¾ teaspoon salt
 ¼ teaspoon dry mustard
 ¼ teaspoon marjoram
 ⅛ teaspoon pepper
 1 tablespoon chopped chives
   Lettuce
 2 medium-sized tomatoes, cut in eighths
   About 2 teaspoons chopped parsley

Reserve three halves of the eggs for garnish. Coarsely chop remaining eggs and place in a bowl with the cottage cheese, salt, mustard, marjoram, pepper, and chopped chives; stir until well blended. Pack into a small bowl to mold. Unmold on a lettuce-lined serving plate, surround with tomato wedges, and sprinkle parsley over the top. Press in the egg halves. Chill at least ½ hour before serving. Makes 4 servings.

Fruit Salad in Romaine Leaves

Make this salad by gently stirring nuts and fruit into cottage cheese; serve with mint dressing.

 1 pint country-style cottage cheese
 ¼ teaspoon seasoned salt
 3 tablespoons mayonnaise
 ½ cup coarsely chopped pecans, cashews, or walnuts
 1½ cups cut-up fruit or whole berries (cantaloupe,
   honeydew melon, fresh peaches, grapes, or
   strawberries)
 6 medium-sized romaine leaves
   Mint Dressing (recipe follows)

Combine cottage cheese, seasoned salt, and mayonnaise. Gently stir in nuts and fruit. Spoon some of the fruit and cheese mixture into each romaine leaf. Arrange filled leaves on a large platter. Serve with Mint Dressing. Makes 6 servings.

MINT DRESSING:

 ½ cup mint jelly
 ¼ cup salad oil
 ¼ teaspoon grated lime peel
 2 or 3 tablespoons lime juice
   Salt

Beat mint jelly with a rotary beater until smooth. Add salad oil, lime peel, lime juice, and a few grains of salt. Stir until blended. Makes about ¾ cup dressing.

Macaroni Cole Slaw

Crisp vegetables combine with macaroni for texture interest in this salad. To make the dish ahead of time, chill the macaroni with the sour cream mixture; chill the vegetables in a separate container and combine all just before serving.

 6 cups cooked elbow or salad macaroni (7 or 8 oz.
   uncooked)
 ½ cup sour cream
 1 teaspoon salt
 ⅛ teaspoon pepper
 3 cups finely shredded cabbage
 1 green pepper, seeded, finely chopped
 1 large carrot, shredded
 3 tablespoons finely chopped onion
 1 clove garlic
 ¼ cup French dressing
 1 tablespoon sugar
 1 teaspoon dry mustard

Cook macaroni as directed on the package; drain well and cool. Combine sour cream with salt and pepper and add to cooled, drained macaroni; stir to coat well, being careful not to mash the macaroni. On top of the macaroni, put the shredded cabbage, green pepper, carrot, and onion; blend in all at once with two forks, the tines of which have been rubbed with a cut surface of the clove of garlic. Combine French dressing with sugar and dry mustard. Add to salad and mix. Makes 8 to 10 servings.

Oriental Luncheon Salad

Rings of green onion and bits of carrot add color to this main dish salad featuring bean sprouts.

  1 pound bean sprouts
1¼ cups steamed rice
  1 cup thinly sliced celery
  2 tablespoons chopped green pepper
  2 small carrots, grated fine
  3 green onions, sliced (include green tops)
  2 cups diced, cooked chicken or pork
½ cup toasted slivered almonds
    Salt and pepper to taste
    Juice of ½ lemon
¾ to 1 cup French dressing
    Lettuce
    Soy sauce

Cook bean sprouts in a small amount of salted water just until crisp-tender, 2 to 3 minutes; drain and allow to cool. In a large bowl, combine bean sprouts, rice, celery, green pepper, carrots, onions, chicken, and almonds. Chill thoroughly. Season with salt, pepper, and lemon juice; pour over French dressing, and mix ingredients lightly. Serve in bowls lined with crisp lettuce. You can pass soy sauce for additional seasoning, if desired. Makes 6 servings.

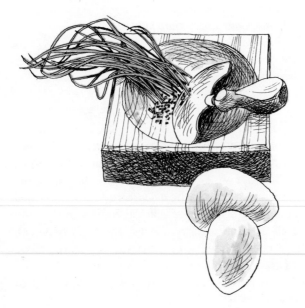

Cottage Cheese, Tomato, Green Bean Salad

This colorful, hearty salad is made from canned and ready-to-eat foods. In the morning, perhaps while preparing breakfast, you will need to put a can of tomato aspic and a can of garlic or onion-seasoned green beans in the refrigerator to chill.

1 can (13½ oz.) tomato aspic, chilled
1 pint (2 cups) cottage cheese, flavored with chives or plain
1 can or jar (1 lb.) garlic or onion-seasoned green beans, chilled
    Lemon wedges for garnish
    Fresh lemon juice

Open chilled tomato aspic and slide aspic from can and cut in thick slices. Arrange on a serving platter. Spoon alongside the aspic the cottage cheese. Thoroughly drain the green beans and arrange beside the cottage cheese. Garnish with lemon wedges and squeeze fresh lemon juice over each serving. Makes 4 to 5 servings.

Macaroni, Bean, and Bacon Salad

Walnuts give a nice crunch to this combination of macaroni and beans, but the crumbled bacon provides the most emphatic flavor. Serve the salad as a cold casserole with broiled or grilled meats.

2 cups cooked elbow macaroni, rinsed in cold water and drained
2 cups cooked or canned kidney beans, drained
¼ cup chopped celery
¼ cup chopped green pepper
¼ cup chopped green onion
1 teaspoon sugar
½ teaspoon salt
    Pepper
5 tablespoons salad oil
3 tablespoons vinegar
½ cup chopped walnuts
    Crisp lettuce leaves
4 slices cooked bacon, crumbled

Combine macaroni, beans, celery, green pepper, onion, sugar, salt, pepper, oil, and vinegar. Blend well. Chill. Stir in walnuts and turn mixture into a lettuce-lined bowl. Sprinkle with bacon. Mix and serve. Makes 6 servings.

Orange-Wheat Salad

Cracked wheat and orange sections are combined in this unusual salad.

1 cup quick-cooking cracked wheat or bulgur
2 tablespoons butter
2 cups water
¼ cup mayonnaise
 Juice of 1 lemon
 Juice of 1 orange
2 teaspoons chopped chives
1 teaspoon sugar
1 teaspoon salt
1 can (11 oz.) mandarin oranges, drained

Brown quick-cooking wheat in the butter in a large saucepan. Add 2 cups water, bring to a boil, cover, and simmer 15 minutes. Remove lid to let steam escape so the cooked wheat will dry a bit.

When cracked wheat is cool, mix to prevent kernels from sticking together, and place in refrigerator until you're ready to add dressing.

Make dressing by mixing together the mayonnaise, lemon juice, orange juice, chives, sugar, and salt. Mix with chilled wheat and orange sections. You might save a few orange sections for a garnish. Makes 4 to 6 servings.

Curried Rice Salad

Curried Rice Salad makes an ideal accompaniment for barbecued lamb or barbecued or fried chicken.

2 cups chilled, cooked rice
1 medium-sized green pepper, shredded
2 tablespoons drained pimientos, cut in strips
2 tablespoons raisins
2 tablespoons chopped parsley
2 tablespoons chopped green onion
½ cup olive oil
⅓ cup wine vinegar
1 tablespoon lemon juice
1 clove garlic, minced or mashed
1 tablespoon sugar
½ teaspoon curry powder
 Salt and pepper to taste
 Salad greens
 Green pepper rings
 Tomato wedges

Using two forks, mix together the rice, green pepper, pimientos, raisins, parsley, and onion. Chill thoroughly.

Combine oil, vinegar, lemon juice, garlic, sugar, curry powder, salt, and pepper. Just before serving, pour over salad and mix thoroughly. Arrange salad in a bowl or casserole. Garnish with crisp greens, green pepper rings, and tomato wedges. Makes 4 servings.

Fruit Salads

FRUITS IN ALL THEIR LOVELY COLORS AND SHAPES

A fruit salad fits gracefully into many menus, and for salad beauty, there is no lovelier choice. Combining fresh fruits in a salad is one of the best ways to show off their beautiful colors and shapes, and when fresh fruits are not in season, canned and frozen fruits make delicious and taste-tempting alternates.

The dressing for a fruit salad is sometimes tossed with the salad ingredients, or it may be served separately. When grapefruit or other juicy fruit is to be mixed with greens, it is a good idea to toss the lettuce with the dressing first and then arrange the fruit over the salad. This will enable the fruit to retain its shape and prevent the juice from diluting the dressing.

A "fruit salad bar" is an eye-catching addition to a buffet table. Serve platters of assorted fruits attractively arranged in rows: thin slices of pineapple; peeled, sliced oranges and grapefruit; grapes, seeded if necessary; sliced pears, bananas, apples, avocado, and papaya dipped in lemon juice to preserve their color. Offer a choice of two or three dressings; French, sour cream, and a thin mayonnaise are good choices. Place chilled salad plates and a bowl of crisp greens nearby, and let guests make their own fruit selections.

Fruits for Salad Tropical are grouped individually to retain their attractive shapes. Cardamom dressing is served on the side. Recipe on page 68.

Stuffed Pear Salad

You may stuff either fresh winter pears or canned Bartletts with this gingersnap and cream cheese filling. The lemon dressing will hold up for several days in your refrigerator, but do not add whipped cream until just before serving.

18 gingersnaps, crushed
½ cup drained crushed pineapple
1 large package (8 oz.) cream cheese
2 tablespoons mayonnaise
4 fresh winter pears or 8 canned pear halves
½ cup sugar
3 tablespoons lemon juice
½ cup orange juice
1 egg, well beaten
¼ teaspoon salt
½ cup whipping cream
*   Lettuce or water cress*

Mix together the crushed gingersnaps, pineapple, cheese, and mayonnaise. Stuff halves of fresh or canned pears with the mixture and chill.

In a double boiler, mix sugar, lemon and orange juice, well-beaten egg, and salt. Cook over hot water until thickened, stirring constantly. When cool, mix with whipped cream. Use as the dressing over the stuffed pears, which have been arranged on crisp lettuce leaves or on sprigs of water cress. Makes 8 servings.

Cranberry Grape Salad

You sugar the ground raw cranberries to draw out their scarlet juice, which literally dyes this salad a rosy red. The juicy Tokays lend a crackling bite.

      1 pound (4 cups) cranberries
1⅔ cups sugar
      2 cups Tokay grapes, halved and seeded
      1 cup sliced celery
      1 cup chopped nut meats
      12 marshmallows, quartered
      ½ pint (1 cup) whipping cream
           Lettuce

Grind cranberries through the fine blade of the food chopper into a medium-sized bowl; add sugar and let stand while you assemble the other ingredients. Add the grapes, celery, nut meats, and marshmallows to the cranberries. Whip cream and fold in thoroughly. Chill for several hours. Serve in lettuce cups. Makes 12 servings.

Fall Fruit and Nut Tray

From fruits in season, such as apples, pears, figs, pineapples, persimmons, bananas, grapes, quinces, guavas, select an assortment of your favorites. Allow 1 or 2 whole fruits, or about 1 cup fruit for each serving. Prepare fruit to eat; peel, pare, seed, and core as is necessary. Cut fruit in about two-bite-size portions (but cut grapes in halves) and arrange each fruit individually in a row on a large tray. Garnish with salted nuts if you wish or serve the nuts in a separate bowl. Let each person select the combination for his own salad. Spoon dressing over each serving.

CHEESE AND NUT DRESSING:

Whip until smooth 1 package (8 oz.) cream cheese with ¼ cup milk and 2 tablespoons lemon juice. Blend ½ cup finely chopped salted macadamia nuts or cashews (or both), 1 cup grated sharp Cheddar cheese, 2 tablespoons sugar, ¼ teaspoon pepper, and salt to taste. Add more milk if you prefer a thinner dressing. Makes about 3 cups.

Stuffed Apple Salad

This can be a sophisticated salad for a buffet, or an amusing one for a children's party. In either case, allow 1 apple for each serving. Slice off the top and carefully scoop out the insides, leaving a thick enough shell so that the apples will hold their shape. Brush cut edges with lemon juice, as well as the cut side of top. Chop pulp to use either of these ways: For adult salad, combine insides of 6 apples with ¼ cup diced marinated herring, ¼ cup diced cooked veal, ¼ cup diced celery. Season with salt and pepper and a little minced onion, and moisten with sour cream. For children's salad, combine pulp with ½ cup chopped dates and ¼ cup chopped nut meats; moisten with mayonnaise.

Fill the apple shells. Using a small round cutter or an apple corer, cut the stems from the apple tops. Place on filled apples; in the holes, stick 3 leaves of Belgian endive or, for the children, 2 or 3 sticks of Cheddar cheese set at jaunty angles. Serve on a pretty platter, garnished with greenery.

Grape Jumble Salad

Four fruits are combined in this salad—grapefruit, grapes, pears, and mandarin oranges.

      Segments from ½ medium-sized grapefruit
1 cup seedless grapes
1 fresh pear, peeled, cored, and diced
1 can (11 oz.) mandarin oranges, drained
4 tablespoons (¼ cup) olive oil or salad oil
1 tablespoon lemon juice
1 tablespoon lime juice
1 teaspoon salt
¼ teaspoon paprika
      Few grains cayenne
      Chicory and water cress

Place grapefruit segments in a bowl with grapes, diced pear, and oranges. Combine olive oil, lemon juice, lime juice, salt, paprika, and cayenne; pour over fruit, and mix together lightly. Chill in refrigerator. Serve on crisp greens. Makes 6 servings.

Grape-Almond Salad with Coriander Dressing

An elusive whiff of ground coriander can be detected in the lemony dressing of this spiced salad.

> Half a head of romaine lettuce
> Half a head of red leaf lettuce
> 1 cup green or seeded red grapes
> ½ cup salted almonds
> 1 can (8 oz.) artichoke hearts, drained
> 6 tablespoons salad oil
> 3 tablespoons lemon juice
> ½ teaspoon dry mustard
> ⅜ teaspoon ground coriander
> ¼ teaspoon salt
> ¼ teaspoon sugar
> ⅛ teaspoon pepper

Into a chilled salad bowl, break the crisp leaves of romaine and red leaf lettuce. Arrange over the greens the grapes and almonds. Peel leaves from artichokes and add to other ingredients. At serving time, mix salad with a dressing made by combining thoroughly the salad oil, lemon juice, dry mustard, ground coriander, salt, sugar, and pepper. Makes about 6 servings.

Apple and Cauliflower Salad

Serve this salad with rich dinner dishes such as roast pork or spareribs, or with a lunch of baked beans and brown bread.

> 4 cups thinly sliced unpeeled Delicious apples
> 1 cup thinly sliced raw cauliflower
> About ¾ cup mayonnaise
> Salt
> Pepper
> Lemon juice (optional)
> Lettuce cups (optional)

Cut apple slices in thirds, crosswise. Mix with cauliflower and enough mayonnaise to coat each piece. Season to taste with salt and pepper. Add a little lemon juice if you like a more tart salad. Chill thoroughly and serve from lettuce cups, if desired. Makes 5 to 6 servings.

Fresh Pear Salad

Serve this salad as a first course with broiled chicken or ham, or with a sandwich for lunch.

> 3 large oranges, peeled, white membrane cut off
> 2 large ripe Comice or Anjou pears, each cut in 6
>   wedges, core removed
> Lemon juice
> Crisp greens
> Lemon French Dressing (recipe follows)

Cut oranges in slices ½ inch thick, about 4 slices to each orange. Sprinkle pears with lemon juice to keep from browning. For each serving, arrange crisp greens on salad plate and top with 3 slices orange and 3 wedges of pear. Spoon 1 to 2 tablespoons of the Lemon French Dressing onto the salad. Makes 4 servings.

LEMON FRENCH DRESSING:

> ⅓ cup lemon juice
> ⅓ cup salad oil
> 2 tablespoons honey
> Dash salt
> ¼ teaspoon finely chopped fresh mint (optional)

Combine lemon juice, salad oil, honey, salt, and mint, if desired. Let stand for at least ½ hour before serving to let flavors combine. Makes about ¾ cup dressing.

Cream cheese dressing with candied ginger accents flavor of plum, pineapple, and grape salad.

Fruit Salad with Ginger-Cream Dressing

A dressing of cream cheese with candied ginger especially enhances the flavor of the plums in this fruit salad.

Arrange fruit on crisp greens on a salad platter or individual salad plates: For each serving, allow 1 slice pineapple (fresh or canned, drained), 1 large or several small plums (cut in halves or quarters), and 1 small bunch seedless grapes.

To make the dressing, blend together 1 small package (3 oz.) cream cheese, 1½ tablespoons sugar, a dash of salt, 2 teaspoons lemon juice, and 1 tablespoon chopped, candied ginger. Spoon a dollop of the dressing over the plums and pineapple. Top each serving with a pecan half, if you wish. Makes enough dressing for about 4 servings.

Pear-Mango Salad

Heaped in the pineapple half shells, this attractive fresh fruit and cottage cheese salad tastes as good as it looks.

> 1 small fresh pineapple
> 1 cup creamed cottage cheese
> 2 pears, peeled and cut in chunks
> 1 mango, peeled and sliced
> 1½ tablespoons sliced preserved ginger
> 1½ tablespoons toasted, sliced Brazil nut meats
>   Sweet French Dressing

Beginning at the crown, cut pineapple in half lengthwise; scoop out the fruit, using a grapefruit knife. In the bottom of each half, place a layer of cottage cheese. Remove core from pineapple fruit which has been cut out and cut fruit into chunks; place a layer over the cottage cheese. Arrange a layer each of pears and mangoes over the pineapple. Top with a sprinkling of ginger and nut meats, and serve with a sweet French dressing. Makes 2 servings as luncheon entrée, or 4 to 6 as side salad.

Salad Tropical

Serve this fruit salad for luncheon with tiny sandwiches of tongue, ham, or proscuitto (the cured Italian ham); or serve the salad after a hearty soup at supper and let it take the place of dessert.

> 1 large pineapple
> 1 large ripe pear
> 1 medium-sized or large papaya
> 1 large ripe Fuerte avocado
> 1 can (1 lb., 4 oz.) litchi nuts, drained
>   Lemon juice
> 2 large tangerines or 1 can (11 oz.) mandarin
>   oranges, drained
> 2 large oranges
>   Lettuce leaves
>   Cardamom Dressing (recipe follows)

Slice top foliage from pineapple and save. Peel the fruit, cut in thick crosswise slices (do not core), and restack slices, topping with the foliage. Set pineapple on a serving tray. Arrange the following fruit around the pineapple in such a way as to retain the identity of each fruit: the unpeeled pear, cored and cut in wedges; the peeled and seeded papaya, cut in wide crosswise slices; the peeled and pitted avocado, cut in lengthwise slices; and the litchis. Brush pear and avocado with lemon juice.

Peel and section the tangerines, removing all white material, and group the pieces on the fruit platter (or use mandarins). Also peel the oranges with a knife, cut in crosswise slices, and place on the tray. Garnish with lettuce. Place a portion of each fruit on individual serving plates and top with the cardamom dressing. Makes 8 servings.

CARDAMOM DRESSING:

Thoroughly beat 1 egg with 1½ tablespoons lemon juice, ⅛ teaspoon ground cardamom, and 1 tablespoon honey. Whip ½ cup heavy cream until stiff; add egg mixture, and continue to beat until mixture is softly whipped. Serve at once. Makes about 2 cups.

Tarragon dressing, topped with sprinkling of tarragon, provides intriguing flavor for sweet plum salad.

Avocado Halves with Hot Cocktail Sauce

For an easy-to-make first course, fill avocado half shells with this heated, spicy sauce which will contrast with the cool, butter-smooth avocado.

4 tablespoons (¼ cup) butter or margarine
4 tablespoons (¼ cup) catsup
2 tablespoons vinegar
2 tablespoons water
1 tablespoon sugar
2 teaspoons Worcestershire
⅓ teaspoon salt
  Dash of liquid hot-pepper seasoning
3 small avocados

In the top of a double boiler, mix together the butter, catsup, vinegar, water, sugar, Worcestershire, salt, and hot-pepper seasoning to taste. Heat over boiling water until butter has melted and sauce is smooth. Cut avocados in half lengthwise, separate halves, and remove seeds. Spoon hot sauce into avocados and serve. Makes 6 servings.

Plum Salad with Tarragon Dressing

This tarragon dressing is most delicious with mild sweet plums.

Cut plums in slices or wedges and arrange on greens on individual salad plates. Top with Tarragon Dressing (recipe follows). If you wish to make the salad in a bowl, gently mix about 6 cups (1½ qt.) of the cut plums with the dressing. Turn into a lettuce-lined bowl and sprinkle top with about 1 teaspoon finely crushed tarragon. Makes 6 servings.

TARRAGON DRESSING:

Blend together ½ cup mayonnaise, 1 tablespoon tarragon white wine vinegar, and 1 teaspoon sugar. Whip ½ cup heavy cream, fold in. Spoon dressing generously over the plums, then sprinkle with finely crushed tarragon. Makes enough dressing for 6 servings.

Bartlett Pear and Tokay Grape Salad

Bartlett pear slices and seeded Tokays are served with slivers of cheese, toasted almonds, and dressing for this salad.

>   Butter lettuce leaves
>   3 or 4 perfectly ripe Bartlett pears, cored and
>   sliced
>   1½ cups seeded Flame Tokay grapes
>   ¼ cup (⅛ lb.) finely diced Fontinella or Edam
>   cheese
>   2 to 3 tablespoons sliced toasted almonds
>   Lemon Honey Dressing (recipe follows)

Line a serving tray with lettuce. Arrange pear slices with grapes on the lettuce. Scatter cheese and almonds over fruit. Moisten with dressing and serve, or top each serving with dressing. Makes 6 to 8 servings.

Bartlett pear slices and seeded Tokays are served with slivers of cheese, toasted almonds, and dressing.

LEMON HONEY DRESSING:

In a small bowl, whisk 1 egg with a fork until white and yolk are blended. Add ¼ cup salad oil and beat until mixed and creamy looking. Stir in 2 tablespoons lemon juice, 2 tablespoons honey, ¼ teaspoon salt, and 2 tablespoons heavy cream. Makes about 1 cup. This is a creamy dressing; if you prefer a thicker mixture, increase the heavy cream to ¼ cup and whip it until stiff before adding to dressing. Makes about 1 cup.

Avocado and Grapefruit Salad

Serve this salad as a first course or with the main part of the meal.

Arrange slices of peeled, pitted, ripe avocado and peeled grapefruit segments on crisp butter lettuce leaves on a large tray or small plates for individual servings. Allow about ⅓ medium-sized avocado and ¼ large grapefruit for each serving. Pour over the fruits enough prepared Italian-style oil and vinegar dressing to moisten.

Orange Salad Cups

You can make Orange Salad Cups ahead and refrigerate them for as long as two hours.

>   3 large oranges, halved (cut with zigzag edges, if
>   desired)
>   1 large red apple, cored and diced
>   ⅓ cup diced celery
>   3 tablespoons mayonnaise
>   ½ teaspoon salt
>   ½ teaspoon sugar
>   6 walnut or pecan halves

Using a grapefruit knife, cut out the pulp of the orange halves. Cut pulp in small pieces and place in small bowl. Combine diced apple with celery and add to orange pieces. Mix together the mayonnaise, salt, and sugar; mix with the fruit and celery mixture. Spoon into the hollowed orange halves; top with a walnut or pecan half and refrigerate until chilled (or up to 2 hours). Makes 6 servings.

DRESSING:

4 small ripe avocados, peeled
  Juice of 2 large limes
4 tablespoons Dijon-style mustard
  About 2 cups mayonnaise
  Pinch of salt
  Shredded zest of orange
  Parsley

Mash avocados gently and blend in lime juice, mustard, enough mayonnaise to make a creamy dressing, and salt. Sprinkle with shredded zest and garnish with parsley. Makes 8 servings.

Grapefruit and Avocado Salad

Early on the day you plan to serve it, prepare the grapefruit for this salad; cover with clear plastic wrap and refrigerate.

Use one pink grapefruit; cut away the peel, including all the white membrane, and remove the sections. Shred 1½ heads crisp lettuce and pile into a salad bowl. Top with grapefruit. Peel and slice one avocado and arrange on salad. Add your favorite French dressing.

Papaya Star Salad

Cheese complements the delicate flavor of papaya in this salad. It is attractive in appearance, too.

2 papayas
1 cup pineapple-cottage cheese
1 small package (3 oz.) cream cheese
¼ teaspoon salt
2 tablespoons lemon juice
  Lettuce
  French dressing or lemon or lime juice

Cut tops from papayas about a quarter of the way down. Carefully scoop out seeds with a teaspoon so as not to spoil the star outline in the center. Combine cottage and cream cheeses, salt, and lemon juice, and mix until smooth. Spoon into papayas, packing down as much as possible. Chill 1 to 2 hours. Cut crosswise in 1½-inch slices, and serve on lettuce or leaf-garnished salad plates with a simple French dressing or a sprinkling of lemon or lime. Makes 4 to 6 servings.

Litchi and Avocado Salad

Avocados are filled with an unusual litchi nut mixture for this salad.

1 can (1 lb., 4 oz.) litchi nuts, chilled
¼ cup lemon juice
¼ cup liquid drained from litchi nuts
¼ cup salad oil
2 tablespoons soy sauce
2 teaspoons grated fresh ginger
6 ripe avocados, cut in halves, pits removed

Open and drain litchi nuts, saving liquid; dice litchi nuts and mix with dressing made by combining lemon juice, liquid from litchi nuts, salad oil, soy sauce, and ginger. Fill avocado halves with the mixture and serve at once. Makes 12 servings.

Oranges with Avocado Dressing

Cut the peel from 8 large oranges, removing all white membrane. Place peel of one orange in saucepan with cold water to cover. Simmer until peel is soft; drain. With a spoon, scrape loosened white pith off peel; finely shred the remaining zest for use in the dressing. Cut each orange in even crosswise slices, keeping slices from each orange together; remove seeds. On a lettuce-lined salad plate, arrange each orange to resemble a whole orange. Top with dressing (recipe follows).

Orange and Green Pepper Salad

Cut the peel from 6 oranges, so that all white is removed, and cut in slices ⅓ inch thick. Arrange in overlapping rows on a platter, surround with lettuce leaves, and top with 1 sweet onion and 1 green pepper, sliced so thinly they are transparent. (You'll need a sharp knife for this, or, if you prefer, just chop the onion and pepper very finely.) Arrange on top of the oranges, pour on a cup of French dressing, and chill thoroughly before serving. Makes 12 servings.

Citrus Salad

You'll have some of this flavorful dressing left for use on other salads.

1 cup salad oil
⅓ cup catsup
½ cup vinegar
1 teaspoon Worcestershire
½ teaspoon salt
  Half a medium onion, chopped or grated
1 large clove garlic, chopped or mashed
1 quart peeled, sliced oranges
2 cans (11 oz. each) mandarin oranges, drained
2 cups thinly sliced sweet onions
1 small can (7 oz.) pitted ripe olives, drained

First make the dressing by combining in your electric blender or a quart jar the salad oil, catsup, vinegar, Worcestershire, salt, onion, and garlic.

(If you use a blender, you can put in the onion and garlic, chopped; otherwise, grate the onion and mash the garlic before adding to the other ingredients.) Whirl or shake until blended.

For the salad, arrange the orange slices, mandarin sections, and onion slices in a serving bowl. Cover with clear plastic wrap or foil, and refrigerate until time to serve. Add dressing at serving time; mix gently. Garnish the salad with whole, pitted olives. Makes 8 servings.

Cherry Fruit Salad

Sesame seed dressing puts the finishing touch on this salad of cantaloupe, pineapple, avocado, cherries, and lettuce.

1 head iceberg lettuce or 2 heads butter lettuce
1 medium-sized cataloupe, peeled and cut in cubes
1 small pineapple, peeled and cut in chunks or 1
  can (1 lb., 13 oz.) pineapple chunks, drained
1 avocado, peeled and diced
1½ cups pitted Bing or Royal Ann cherries
½ teaspoon salt
  Juice of ½ lemon

DRESSING:

2 tablespoons sesame seed
1 cup (½ pint) sour cream
  Juice of 1 lime
3 tablespoons undiluted frozen orange juice
  concentrate
¼ teaspoon salt

Line a salad bowl with lettuce cups and tear the remaining greens into bite-sized chunks. Lightly mix together the lettuce chunks with the cantaloupe, pineapple, avocado, cherries, salt, and lemon juice. Pile in the salad bowl; chill.

For the dressing, sprinkle the sesame seed in a shallow pan and toast in a moderate oven (350°) for 10 minutes, or until golden brown. Mix together the sour cream, lime juice, orange juice concentrate, salt, and toasted sesame seed. Serve in a separate dish to accompany the salad. Makes 6 servings.

Ensalada de Naranjas (Orange Salad)

The refreshing flavor of oranges will make this salad a welcome contrast to other foods on your menu. It goes especially well with Mexican food.

5 large oranges, peeled and thinly sliced
1 white onion, peeled and thinly sliced
⅓ cup salad oil
¼ cup wine vinegar
1 teaspoon sugar
½ teaspoon salt
¼ teaspoon chili powder
Paprika
Lettuce (optional)

Arrange orange and onion slices in a bowl, distributing the onions throughout the oranges. Pour over a dressing of oil, vinegar, sugar, salt, and chili powder. Sprinkle with paprika. If you wish, serve on crisp lettuce. Makes 8 servings.

Papaya, Orange, and Avocado Salad

This salad offers the unusual combination of papaya, orange, and avocado with a chili dressing.

Peel 1 papaya; cut in halves or quarters and remove seeds. Peel 3 medium-sized oranges, cutting away white membrane; slice thinly crosswise, removing as many seeds as possible. Peel, cut in halves, and pit 2 ripe avocados. Let fruit marinate several hours in Chili Dressing (recipe follows) in refrigerator; drain and arrange on tray. Offer dressing with each serving. Makes 4 servings.

CHILI DRESSING:

Combine ¼ cup salad oil, ¼ cup lemon juice, 1 tablespoon finely minced dry or green onion, ½ teaspoon chili powder, ½ teaspoon salt, and ¼ teaspoon freshly ground black pepper.

Hot Spiced Fruit Salad

The canned and fresh fruits in this salad are poached in a syrup that's seasoned with butter and spices. It especially complements turkey or ham.

1 can (1 lb.) peach halves
1 can (1 lb.) pear halves
1 can (1 lb.) apricot halves
1 can (1 lb.) pineapple chunks
1 can (1 lb.) pitted light sweet cherries
2 tart apples, peeled, cored, and cubed
Juice of 1 lemon
½ teaspoon nutmeg
½ teaspoon cinnamon
¼ teaspoon ground cloves
⅓ cup brown sugar, firmly packed
¼ cup (⅛ lb.) butter or margarine
2 cups fresh seedless grapes or halved seeded grapes
3 bananas, peeled and cut in chunks
Sour cream or whipped cream (optional)

Drain the syrup from all the canned fruits; measure and reserve 1½ cups of the combined fruit syrup. Turn the drained, canned fruits and the apple cubes into a covered baking dish or casserole (2½ quart size). Sprinkle lemon juice over fruit. To the 1½ cups fruit syrup add the nutmeg, cinnamon, cloves, and brown sugar; pour over fruit. Dot top of fruit with pieces of the butter.

Cover baking dish and put in a moderate oven (350°) for 20 minutes.. Remove the dish from the oven and lightly stir in the grapes and bananas. Cover and continue baking for 5 minutes. Serve hot, either plain or with sour cream or whipped cream. Makes 12 servings.

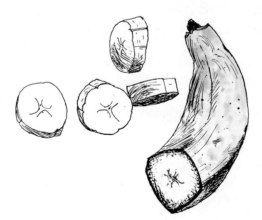

Casaba Melon Salad

You marinate diced chunks and crescents of casaba melon along with dates in a light low-calorie dressing to make this salad.

½ *medium-large chilled casaba melon, seeds removed*
¾ *cup pitted dates, cut in pieces*
  2 *tablespoons lime juice*
  2 *tablespoons water*
  2 *tablespoons sauterne*
  1 *tablespoon sugar*
  1 *tablespoon light or dark rum*
  Lime slices

Cut 5 lengthwise crescents of melon; the widest point in the center of each should be about 1½ inches. Cut off the rind and cut each crescent in half crosswise. Lay sections flat in one side of a flat, rimmed dish. Cut fruit from remaining section of melon and dice. Combine with dates and place fruit alongside the crescents. Blend together lime juice, water, wine, sugar, and rum. Pour over fruits; cover and chill.

To serve, set crescents in a ring, so that the narrow tips point out and upward (it may be necessary to slice a little piece from the base of each crescent to make it sit steady). Mound melon pieces and dates in the center of the ring. Drizzle with some of the marinade and garnish with lime slices. Makes 5 or 6 servings.

Pineapple Salad with Roquefort Dressing

Roquefort dressing and paprika top this salad combination of pineapple and shrimp.

¼ *cup crumbled Roquefort cheese*
  1 *cup sour cream*
¼ *cup mayonnaise*
  Dash of salt
  2 *to 3 tablespoons light cream*
  Fruit from 1 large fresh pineapple, cut in quarter slices or finger shapes
¾ *pound cooked, shelled shrimp (if large, cut in pieces)*
  Romaine leaves
  Paprika

Marinated crescents of casaba melon stand in a ring on tray; melon and date mixture fills center.

Mash cheese with back of a spoon or fork until soft. Blend in sour cream until smooth. Stir in mayonnaise, salt, and cream. Makes about 1½ cups dressing.

Combine fruit with shrimp. Mix lightly. Arrange romaine leaves on each salad plate. Top with pineapple mixture. Spoon dressing over and sprinkle with paprika. Makes 6 to 8 servings.

Fresh Persimmon Salad

The sweet and slightly astringent persimmon is good with cucumber or avocado in a fruit salad.

Arrange slices of cucumber or avocado on crisp lettuce on individual salad plates. Top each serving with a spoonful of ripe persimmon pulp. Garnish with wedges of lime or lemon; serve a mild creamy dressing if you wish.

Crenshaw and Persian Melon Appetizer Salad

Pile various sized balls of Persian and Crenshaw melon into a serving dish and chill with a lime-spice dressing to make this salad. It is good served as a salad or dessert.

1 medium-sized Crenshaw melon
1·medium-sized Persian melon
2 tablespoons lime juice (or juice of 1 large lime)
2 tablespoons honey
¼ teaspoon ground coriander
¼ teaspoon nutmeg

Cut melons in halves, remove and discard seeds. Cut fruit into balls of different sizes, using melon (or French) ball cutter, or metal measuring spoons. Place fruit and all juices in a deep bowl. Mix together lime juice, honey, coriander, and nutmeg. Blend with the melon. Cover and chill. Spoon into serving bowls. Makes 8 to 10 servings.

Persian and Crenshaw melon balls are chilled with lime-spice dressing to make refreshing appetizer salad.

Tomato and Cantaloupe Ball Salad

Cantaloupe half shells serve as the bowls for this simple, good-looking salad.

1 cantaloupe, cut in half, seeds removed
2 tomatoes, stem ends trimmed, cut in wedges
½ cup French dressing
  Salt and pepper to taste
2 sprigs mint (optional)
  Endive
2 lime wedges (optional)

Scoop cantaloupe pulp into balls. Mix together the cantaloupe balls and tomato wedges and refill each half shell. Pour over French dressing, and sprinkle with salt and pepper to taste; garnish with mint. Serve on a bed of endive. Garnish each salad with a wedge of lime. Makes 2 servings.

Fruit Salad with Pecan Dressing

Nut meats are mixed in this tart salad dressing. Sliced papaya would make a good addition to the fresh fruit combination.

½ cup salad oil
¼ cup orange juice
1 tablespoon lemon juice
1 teaspoon sugar
¼ teaspoon salt
¼ cup finely chopped, toasted pecan meats
1 cup cubed fresh or canned pineapple
2 bananas, sliced
1 cup seedless grapes
2 pears, peeled and diced
2 red-skinned apples, diced

Pour salad oil and orange juice into a 1-pint screw top jar or plastic shaker. Add lemon juice, sugar, salt, and chopped nut meats. (If you toast pecan meats in a moderate oven (350°) for 10 minutes, they are more crisp and flavorful.) Cover tightly and shake until dressing is mixed thoroughly. Makes 1 cup dressing. Mix together chilled pineapple, sliced bananas, grapes, diced pears, and diced apples. Pour dressing over fruit and mix lightly. Makes 6 servings.

Molded & Frozen Salads

FESTIVE, MAKE-AHEAD, EASY ON THE HOSTESS

Molded and frozen salads are, for the most part, quite simple to make, yet they present a very festive picture. Encasing salad ingredients in a shimmering, sparkling gelatin or creamy-smooth base seems to give them a new personality. Even the simplest molded or frozen salad has a special party air about it, and these salads have one characteristic that makes them favorites of busy homemakers and hostesses—they must be made ahead, at least two hours or more before they are to be served.

In deciding which molded or frozen salad to include in a meal, be guided by the general rules of menu harmony. The rich, mousse-type molded or frozen salad is hearty fare and should be served with simple dishes. Spicy salads, in individual molds, make good meat accompaniments. Other salads in this chapter double as desserts.

Here are some things to remember when unmolding gelatin salads. The salad should be chilled thoroughly, preferably overnight. To break the vacuum that holds the salad to the mold, gently slide the pointed tip of a knife in at one edge to a depth of about half an inch. Unmold by dipping the mold in lukewarm water, or by inverting the mold on a serving plate and covering it with a warm cloth.

Whole berries show on surface of Boysenberry-Nut Salad. Creamy Asparagus Salad appears at left. Recipes on pages 79, 82, and 83.

Frozen Apple Salad

Consider this frozen fruit salad for a holiday dinner. It can be made well ahead.

1 can (9 oz.) crushed pineapple, drained well, syrup reserved
2 eggs, slightly beaten
½ cup sugar
Dash salt
3 tablespoons lemon juice
2 cups finely chopped unpared apples
½ cup finely spliced celery
1 cup whipping cream
Crisp salad greens
Red-skinned apple slices for garnish
Lemon juice

Measure the pineapple syrup and add water, if needed, to make ½ cup liquid. In a pan, combine the eggs, sugar, salt, lemon juice, and syrup mixture. Cook over low heat, stirring constantly, until thickened; chill. Stir the pineapple, chopped apples, and celery into the chilled custard mixture; whip the cream and fold in carefully. Pour into two refrigerator freezing trays or into a 1½-quart baking dish. Cover well and freeze until firm.

When you are ready to serve it, cut in squares and serve on individual plates. Garnish with greens and the slices of apples, which you first rub with lemon juice. Makes 8 to 10 servings.

Pineapple-Cheese Salad

This salad can be made in one large six-cup mold or six to eight small ones.

2 envelopes unflavored gelatin
½ cup cold water
2½ cups (1 lb. can) crushed pineapple
3 tablespoons lemon juice
½ cup sugar
1 cup heavy cream, whipped
1 cup shredded Cheddar cheese
½ cup chopped walnuts

Soften the gelatin in cold water. Heat the crushed pineapple (do not drain) and stir in the softened gelatin until dissolved. Add the lemon juice and sugar; chill until mixture is partially set. Then fold in the whipped cream, cheese, and nuts. Pour into molds and chill until set. To serve, unmold and garnish with walnut halves. Makes 6 to 8 servings.

Individual pineapple-cheese molds have whipped cream folded into the other ingredients.

Orange Sherbet Salad or Dessert

Orange sherbet dissolved in orange-flavored gelatin makes a rich mold with good orange flavor. Serve it with a creamy dressing.

3 packages (3 oz. each) orange-flavored gelatin
2½ cups boiling water
3 cans (11 oz. each) mandarin orange sections, drained, liquid reserved
1 pint orange sherbet
3 bananas

Dissolve the gelatin in the boiling water. Add 1½ cups of the drained orange liquid to the gelatin. Stir in the sherbet until dissolved and refrigerate until partially set. Peel and slice the bananas and add to the thickened gelatin along with the drained oranges. Pour into a 6-cup mold and chill until set. Makes 6 to 8 servings.

Grapefruit-Cream Cheese Mold

Use regular or pink grapefruit in this salad. For a brighter pink color, add red food coloring.

2 envelopes unflavored gelatin
½ cup cold water
1 cup boiling water
⅓ cup sugar
¾ teaspoon salt
3 cups fresh grapefruit pieces and juice (with all rind and membrane removed)
Few drops red food coloring (optional)
1 large package (8 oz.) cream cheese
2 tablespoons light cream
1 tablespoon sugar
Dash salt
1 cup chopped pecans
Fresh berries or pomegranate seeds (optional)

Soften the gelatin in the cold water; add the boiling water and stir until gelatin is dissolved. Add the ⅓ cup sugar, ¾ teaspoon salt, grapefruit, and food coloring (if used). Pour half of this mixture into a 6-cup ring mold and refrigerate until set. Beat the cream cheese with the cream, 1 tablespoon sugar, and dash salt. Stir in the nuts and

Meanwhile, cut apricots into ½-inch cubes and add to the reserved gelatin mixture. Whip the cottage cheese until smooth and fold into the apricot-gelatin mixture. When the grape-gelatin layer in the mold has set, pour the cottage cheese-apricot-gelatin mixture on top of it in the mold to make the creamy bottom layer. Chill until firm, at least 2 hours. Unmold onto serving dish. Garnish with crisp greens, if you wish. This salad does not need a dressing. Makes 6 servings.

Boysenberry Nut Salad

Boysenberries and nuts add color and texture to this festive fruit salad mold. Serve the Honey-Cream Dressing in a small bowl to spoon over individual servings.

1 package (10 oz.) frozen boysenberries, thawed, drained, liquid reserved
  Water
1 package (3 oz.) lemon-flavored gelatin
¼ cup sherry
1 small can (6 oz.) evaporated milk, chilled
½ cup chopped walnuts
  Crisp greens for garnish
  Honey-Cream Dressing (recipe follows)

Measure boysenberry liquid and add enough water to make 1 cup. Heat the 1 cup liquid to boiling and add the lemon gelatin, stirring until dissolved. Add sherry. Cool, then chill until thick and syrupy (about 30 minutes). Whip the chilled evaporated milk and fold into gelatin mixture. Fold in the boysenberries and nuts. Turn into a 1-quart salad mold or 8 individual molds (½-cup size). Chill until firm, at least 2 hours. Unmold onto serving plate, garnish with crisp greens, and serve with Honey-Cream Dressing. Makes 6 to 8 servings.

HONEY-CREAM DRESSING:

Mix together 1 cup sour cream, 2 teaspoons honey, and 2 teaspoons lemon juice until well blended. Chill and serve. For those who are counting calories, you may substitute yogurt for the sour cream.

spread over the set layer of gelatin. Pour the remaining gelatin into the mold and refrigerate until set. Garnish with fresh berries or pomegranate seeds, if you wish. Makes 8 servings.

Grape and Apricot Mold

To make this two-layer salad, mold the gelatin mixtures one at a time, first the clear top layer with grapes, then the creamy bottom layer with apricots.

2 packages (3 oz. each) lemon-flavored gelatin
2 cups boiling water
3 tablespoons lemon juice
1 can (about 9 oz.) grapes, drained and halved
½ cup cold water
1 can (1 lb.) apricot halves, drained
1 cup small curd creamed cottage cheese
  Crisp greens (optional)

Dissolve gelatin in boiling water; stir in lemon juice. Cool, then chill until thick and syrupy (about 30 minutes). Mix the grapes and cold water into 1 cup of the chilled gelatin mixture. Pour into a 1½-quart salad mold, or into 6 large (1-cup size) individual molds, or 12 small (½-cup) individual molds. Chill until gelatin is quite firm but not completely set (about 1 hour).

Melon Ball-Grape Salad

Two distinct grape flavors blend in this molded salad, which is served with watermelon balls.

3 cups grape juice
2 packages (3 oz. each) lemon-flavored gelatin
¼ cup lime juice or lemon juice
3 cups cut and seeded red grapes
  Salad greens (optional)
2 cups watermelon balls
¼ cup red wine (optional)
  Sour cream

In a saucepan, heat the grape juice (if you use concentrated juice, dilute it as directed on the can). Add gelatin to the hot grape juice and stir until thoroughly dissolved; stir in the lime juice. Chill until syrupy, then stir in the grapes and turn into a ring mold or other salad mold (about 2-quart size). Chill until firm. To serve, unmold on a plate, garnish with greens, if you wish. Fill the center of the ring with the melon balls that have been sprinkled with wine and chilled about 1 hour, or use plain melon balls. (If you use a mold of a different shape, surround it on the plate with the melon.) Serve with sour cream for the dressing. Makes 6 to 8 servings.

Avocado-Beet Salad

Make the gelatin mixture for this Avocado-Beet Salad several hours in advance and refrigerate it. Shortly before serving, spoon it into prepared avocado halves.

1 can (1 lb.) sliced beets, drained, liquid reserved
1 envelope unflavored gelatin
1 cup orange juice
2 tablespoons mayonnaise
¾ teaspoon salt
¼ teaspoon pepper
4 avocados, peeled and halved
  Juice of 1 lemon
  Lettuce leaves
  Mayonnaise dressing
  Parsley

Put beet liquid in a small saucepan and bring to a boil. Soften gelatin in ½ cup of the orange juice; add the boiling beet liquid, stirring to dissolve gelatin. Put mixture in an electric blender, add beets, remaining orange juice, mayonnaise, salt, and pepper; whirl until smooth. Pour into a bowl and refrigerate until set, at least 2 hours. Shortly before serving time, prepare avocados and coat each with lemon juice. Place each half on a lettuce leaf and arrange on serving tray. Using a serving spoon, make large scoops from beet gelatin and place in the hollowed avocado centers. Place a bowl of mayonnaise in the center of the tray and garnish with parsley. Refrigerate until ready to serve. Makes 8 servings.

Roquefort Mold with Shrimp

This smooth cheese mold makes a pretty center and provides a creamy dressing for a platter of shrimp and relishes.

1 package (4 oz.) Roquefort cheese
½ cup sour cream
2 tablespoons lemon juice
¼ teaspoon salt
¼ teaspoon garlic salt
1 envelope unflavored gelatin
¼ cup cold water
½ pint (1 cup) whipping cream
  Greens (romaine, iceberg, or butter lettuce)
1 pound cooked small ocean shrimp or 3 cans (5 oz. each) shrimp
1 cucumber, scored with fork, sliced thinly
1 cup cherry tomatoes
6 to 8 marinated artichoke hearts
  Water cress for garnish
  French or Thousand Island Dressing (optional)

Cream cheese until light and fluffy and blend in sour cream, lemon juice, salt, and garlic salt. Soften gelatin in cold water and dissolve over hot water. Slowly pour liquid gelatin into the creamed cheese and beat until smooth. Whip cream until stiff and fold in. Turn into a 1-quart melon mold or other mold and chill until firm.

Turn out on an oval platter lined with greens. Arrange shrimp on both sides of the mold. Arrange sliced cucumbers, cherry tomatoes, and artichoke hearts at the ends of the platter. Garnish with sprigs of water cress. If you wish, pass French or Thousand Island Dressing. Makes 6 servings.

Tangy Tuna Salad

Celery-flavored gelatin is the base of this molded main-dish luncheon salad.

2 packages (3 oz. each) celery-flavored gelatin
2 cups boiling water
½ cup lemon juice
1 cup cold water
1 cup sliced celery
2 cans (6½ oz. each) tuna, drained and flaked
1 cup cottage cheese
⅓ cup sliced pimiento-stuffed olives
   Lettuce
   Mayonnaise thinned with small amount of fresh
     lemon juice (optional)
   Tomato wedges or slices (optional)
   Hard-cooked eggs (optional)
   Olives for garnish (optional)

Combine the gelatin and boiling water and stir until thoroughly dissolved. Stir in the lemon juice and cold water. Put the gelatin into the refrigerator to chill until it becomes thick and syrupy. Stir in the sliced celery, tuna, cottage cheese, and the sliced olives.

Pour the mixture into 8 to 10 individual salad molds or into a 2-quart mold. Chill overnight, or until the gelatin is firmly set.

To serve, unmold and garnish the serving plate or individual salad plates with lettuce. Offer mayonnaise thinned with lemon juice for those who wish it. You could also garnish each salad plate with tomatoes, hard-cooked eggs, and olives. Makes about 8 to 10 servings.

Mustard Ring

Here is an excellent salad-relish accompaniment for ham. For contrast to the smooth texture of the mustard-flavored ring mold, fill the center with a cabbage slaw.

4 eggs
¾ cup sugar
1 envelope unflavored gelatin
1½ tablespoons dry mustard
½ teaspoon turmeric
¼ teaspoon salt
1 cup water
½ cup cider vinegar
½ pint (1 cup) whipping cream
   Cole slaw (optional)
   Pineapple chunks, frozen or canned, or diced
     pears (optional)
   Greens

Beat eggs in top of double boiler. Mix together thoroughly the sugar and unflavored gelatin; stir in mustard, turmeric, and salt. Add the water and vinegar to the eggs, stir in the sugar mixture, and cook over boiling water until slightly thickened, stirring continuously. Cool until it is thick. Whip cream and fold in. Turn into a 1½-quart ring mold. When firm, unmold and, if desired, fill center with cole slaw to which you might add frozen or canned pineapple chunks or diced winter pears. Garnish with chicory, cress, or other feathery greens. Makes 8 servings.

Mold tender asparagus tips in clear chicken-flavored aspic to make this handsome first course dish.

Asparagus Tips in Aspic

Mold tender asparagus tips in clear chicken-flavored aspic for this first course salad. You can begin preparation the day before.

2 cans (14 oz. each) chicken broth
1 pound bony chicken pieces
3 medium-sized carrots, chopped
2 medium-sized onions, sliced
1 lemon, sliced
1 teaspoon tarragon
4 egg whites, beaten slightly
1 envelope unflavored gelatin
¼ cup cold water
24 to 30 asparagus tips
  Boiling salted water or chicken broth
6 wedges of thin lemon slices
  Parsley
  Sour Cream

In a large pan, combine the 2 cans of chicken broth, chicken pieces, carrots, onions, lemon, and

tarragon. Bring to a boil and simmer gently, covered, for 50 minutes. Pour mixture through a wire strainer. Discard bones and vegetables. Chill broth (overnight if desired). Skim off solidified fat; discard.

Bring stock to a boil, and whisk in the egg whites and cook until stock resumes boiling. Remove from heat and let stand 1 or 2 minutes. Moisten a muslin cloth in cold water and wring dry. Line a large wire strainer with the cloth. Pour liquid through it; drain well (don't squeeze cloth). Discard egg white.

Measure stock; reserve 3 cups (save any extra for other uses such as cooking the asparagus). Soften gelatin in cold water, then dissolve over hot water and blend with stock. Cover and keep at room temperature.

Cut asparagus tips to fit individual molds (5-oz. custard cups or the classic egg-in-aspic mold), measuring to arrange tips horizontally. Cook asparagus in a wide pan in boiling salted water or chicken broth to cover, until it is just tender enough to pierce easily with tip of a sharp knife. Drain and chill.

Pour about ½ inch of the stock into each of 6 small molds and chill until set. Place a slice of lemon wedge on each aspic layer and top each with 1 or 2 asparagus tips. Pour in additional stock almost to cover spears. (If stock gels, warm over hot water to soften, but do not add to molds if warm.)

Chill again until aspic is set. Add 3 or 4 more tips to each mold, and again add stock barely to cover. Chill until set. Fill molds equally with the remaining stock. Chill again until set (covered if to be kept overnight). Dip molds in hot water briefly to loosen aspic. Unmold on individual plates or a tray. Garnish with sprigs of parsley. Offer sour cream to serve as a dressing with asparagus in aspic. Makes 6 servings.

Asparagus Salad

The smooth base for this salad is cream of asparagus soup with chopped celery for crunch. Serve as a beginning course to take the place of soup; pass Lemon-Yogurt Dressing.

2 envelopes unflavored gelatin
½ cup cold water
1 can (10½ oz.) cream of asparagus soup

1 cup water
1 tablespoon lemon juice
1 cup mayonnaise
1 cup finely diced celery
   Parsley for garnish
   Lemon-Yogurt Dressing (recipe follows)

Soften gelatin in the ½ cup cold water. Mix the soup with the 1 cup water until well blended; heat to boiling. Add the softened gelatin to soup mixture, stir until gelatin is dissolved, and add lemon juice. Cool, then chill until syrupy (about 30 minutes). Fold in the mayonnaise and celery and turn into a 1-quart salad mold or 8 individual molds (½-cup size). Chill until firm, at least 2 hours. Unmold; garnish with parsley. Serve with Lemon-Yogurt Dressing. Makes 8 servings.

LEMON-YOGURT DRESSING:

Mix 1 cup plain yogurt or sour cream with 1 teaspoon lemon juice and ⅛ teaspoon seasoned salt. Serve with Asparagus Salad.

Pineapple-Onion Salad

Serve this festive salad with a special ham dinner.

   1 envelope unflavored gelatin
   ½ cup pineapple juice (or syrup from
      canned pineapple tidbits)
   1½ cups boiling water
   1 tablespoon lemon juice
   ½ cup sugar
   1 can (about 14 oz.) pineapple tidbits, drained
   ½ can (3¼ oz.) capers, drained
   1 can (3½ oz.) tiny pickled onions, drained
   3 tablespoons chopped pimiento
      Lettuce
      Mayonnaise

Dissolve gelatin in pineapple juice; add boiling water, lemon juice, and sugar. Allow to set until thickened, but still runny. Stir in pineapple tidbits, capers, pickled onions, and pimiento. Pour mixture into either 6 individual molds or a 1-quart mold. Just before serving, unmold on crisp lettuce and garnish with mayonnaise. Makes 6 servings.

Molded Gazpacho Salad

The ingredients usually used in the Spanish cold soup, *gazpacho*, are used here in a molded salad. It makes a nice summer meal with cold cuts and hot rolls.

   1 envelope unflavored gelatin
      About 1½ cups tomato juice
   1 large ripe tomato
   2 tablespoons vinegar or pickle juice
   ⅛ teaspoon crushed garlic
   1 medium-sized cucumber, chopped
   1 peeled and seeded green chili, chopped
   ¼ cup chopped onion
   ¾ teaspoon salt
   ⅛ teaspoon freshly ground pepper
      Greens

Soften the gelatin in ¼ cup of the tomato juice for about 5 minutes. Meanwhile heat 1 cup of the tomato juice; add the gelatin and stir until thoroughly dissolved. Chop the fresh tomato, saving the juice; add vinegar and remaining tomato juice to make ½ cup liquid. Add to the hot mixture with the garlic, cucumber, green chili, onion, salt and pepper. Pour into a 1-quart mold. Chill until firm. Unmold on crisp greens. Makes 4 to 6 servings.

Tomato Aspic with Vegetables

Serve this full-bodied tomato aspic as a dinner salad or garnished with shrimp as an entrée. A creamy dressing, perhaps flavored with lemon or horse-radish, makes the best flavor complement.

    3 envelopes unflavored gelatin
    ¾ cup cold water
    2½ cups tomato juice
    1 can (6 oz.) tomato paste
    ¼ cup vinegar
    3 tablespoons lemon juice
    1½ teaspoon basil
    1 teaspoon salt
    1 teaspoon sugar
    ⅛ teaspoon onion powder
    ⅛ teaspoon black pepper
    ½ teaspoon Worcestershire
    1 cup chopped celery
    ½ cup chopped green pepper
    1 avocado, diced
    1 can (2¼ oz.) pitted sliced ripe olives
        Cooked, chilled shrimp for garnish (optional)

Soften gelatin in the cold water. Bring 1 cup of the tomato juice to a boil; stir in the gelatin until dissolved. Add the remaining tomato juice, the tomato paste, vinegar, lemon juice, basil, salt, sugar, onion powder, black pepper, and Worcestershire. Refrigerate until partially thickened. Stir in the celery, green pepper, avocado, and olives. Pour into a 6-cup mold; refrigerate until set. Unmold and garnish with shrimp, if you wish. Makes 6 to 8 servings.

Crab Aspic Salad

To serve this salad as a main dish, garnish each portion with half an avocado, sliced.

    2 envelopes unflavored gelatin
    ½ cup cold water
    ¾ cup chili sauce
    ¾ cup water
    ⅔ cup rose wine or tomato juice
    ½ cup sour cream
    1 tablespoon instant minced onion
    ½ teaspoon dill weed or dill seed

Rich, red tomato aspic is filled with celery, green pepper, avocado, and ripe olives. Tomato juice and tomato paste are both included in the recipe to produce full-bodied flavor. Shrimps garnish the plate.

¾ teaspoon salt
1 tablespoon lemon juice
1 can (2¼ oz.) sliced ripe olives, drained
4 hard-cooked eggs
1½ cups fresh, frozen, or canned crab meat
   Salad greens
   Sour cream or mayonnaise dressing (optional)

Soften the gelatin in the cold water. Heat the chili sauce and ¾ cup water in a pan; add gelatin mixture and stir until dissolved. Remove from heat and stir in the wine or tomato juice, sour cream, onion, dill, salt, and lemon juice. Chill until it begins to set.

Set aside a few of the olive slices for garnish. Also cut 2 of the eggs into wedges or slices to use for garnish. Chop remaining two eggs and add to gelatin with remaining olive slices and crab. Turn into a 6-cup mold, or into 6 or 8 small molds. Chill. Unmold on greens; garnish with egg and olive slices. Pass sour cream or mayonnaise dressing, if you wish. Makes 6 to 8 servings.

Sole Mousse with Shrimp

This deliciously flavored and beautifully decorated dish provides a convenient and gracious way to serve a buffet dinner party to twelve guests.

  2 cups dry white wine
  1 onion, thinly sliced
  1 carrot, thinly sliced
  2 sprigs parsley
  1 teaspoon salt
  8 to 10 whole black peppers
2½ pounds boneless sole fillets
  2 envelopes unflavored gelatin
  1 small onion, minced
  3 tablespoons butter
  2 tablespoons flour
1½ cups light cream
   Salt
   Juice of 1 lemon
  2 teaspoons prepared mustard
  2 cups heavy cream, whipped stiff
  1 pound small, cooked, deveined shrimp
  1 cucumber, thinly sliced

In a wide shallow pan, combine wine, sliced onion and carrot, parsley, salt, and whole black peppers. Cover, bring to a boil, and simmer about 5 minutes. Poach the fish fillets in this stock a few at a time; cook 2 to 3 minutes, or until fish flakes. Lift fillets from stock with slotted spatula and place together in a pan. When all are cooked, drain into the stock any juice from pan holding the fish. Strain stock and save, you should have 2 cups (add water to make this total if necessary). Grind fish through fine blade of a food chopper or whirl until smooth in a blender, using some of the stock to make a smooth paste.

Cool ½ cup of the stock, add gelatin and set aside to soften. Meanwhile cook minced onion in butter until soft, but not browned. Stir in flour, blend in light cream. Cook, stirring, until thickened. Remove from heat, salt to taste, stir in gelatin mixture until dissolved. Add fish, lemon juice, any remaining stock, and the mustard. Chill until partially set; fold in whipped cream. Pour into a straight sided, flat bottomed, round or square 3-quart mold. Cover and chill overnight.

To serve, unmold on a platter, decorate with shrimp and cucumber slices. Spoon extra shrimp over each serving. Makes 12 to 14 servings.

Beautifully decorated Sole Mousse with Shrimp stars at buffet dinner for twelve special guests.

Salad Dressings

FOR THE FINAL FLAVOR BALANCE

A salad dressing gives the final flavor balance to a salad. It should point up and blend the flavors of the salad ingredients. Most vegetables, greens, meats, seafood, and eggs need a piquant dressing to set off their flavors to best advantage. On the other hand, some tart fruits take kindly to the addition of a creamy, sweet dressing. But there is no one "compulsory" dressing for any one salad; it is a matter of individual tastes, and variety is the key to good eating.

Often the ingredients that comprise the dressing for a green salad are added directly to the greens and gently mixed in. This classic method of dressing a mixed green salad is discussed on page 6, where you'll also find some suggested recipes for dressings to use in this way. Others of the salads in this book call for their own dressing to be mixed separately and added shortly before serving.

The salad dressing recipes in this chapter include variations of classic mayonnaise or oil-and-vinegar French dressings. Also given are special recipes for dressings you make in a blender. A number of these recipes are for low calorie dressings, with ingredients such as yogurt, buttermilk, or mashed avocado replacing all or part of the oil.

Herbed mayonnaise for greens and shellfish is made at table in two minutes or less. Other ingredients are ready to add. Recipe on pages 52 and 53.

Barbara Worth Salad Dressing

Make this dressing far enough ahead to allow it to ripen several hours.

1 large clove garlic
2 teaspoons salt
1 cup olive oil or salad oil
½ cup red wine vinegar
½ cup heavy cream
1 tablespoon sesame seed
Freshly ground black pepper to taste

Dice garlic on a chopping board; sprinkle with salt, then work salt and garlic together, using the flat blade of a table knife, until garlic is completely blended with salt. Combine with remaining ingredients; stir well or shake in a jar. Allow dressing to ripen for several hours, and stir or shake well just before using. Makes 4 cups dressing.

Lemon Cream Dressing

This salad dressing, although it seems very rich, contains fewer calories than an equal measure of oil and vinegar or a mayonnaise dressing. Use it with delicate greens such as butter lettuce or limestone lettuce.

Blend ½ cup heavy cream, 2 tablespoons lemon juice, ¼ teaspoon salt, and a dash of pepper. Makes enough dressing for 6 to 8 cups greens.

Blender French Dressing

The advantage of using your blender to make French dressing is that flavoring ingredients can be added whole; they are chopped and mixed in the few seconds it takes to whirl them in the blender. Avoid overblending French dressing, for it will become aerated rapidly. This basic garlic-flavored dressing is followed by three variations.

⅓ cup wine vinegar
1 clove garlic
1 teaspoon salt
¼ teaspoon pepper
1 cup olive oil or salad oil

Put the vinegar, garlic, salt, and pepper in the blender and whirl until the garlic clove is finely chopped. Add oil and whirl about 20 seconds longer. Makes about 1⅓ cups dressing.

ANCHOVY FRENCH DRESSING:

Add 3 or 4 anchovy fillets or 1 tablespoon anchovy paste with the oil and whirl until smooth.

BLUE CHEESE FRENCH DRESSING:

Add 3 tablespoons blue cheese with the oil and whirl until the cheese is in very small bits.

CAPER FRENCH DRESSING:

Add 1½ to 2 tablespoons capers with the vinegar and complete as directed in the French dressing recipe above.

Vinaigrette Dressing

Serve this dressing with cold asparagus, broccoli, or salad greens.

2 hard-cooked egg yolks
¼ cup malt vinegar
6 tablespoons salad oil
2 green onions, finely chopped
Salt and coarse black pepper to taste

Mash yolks to a paste with vinegar; gradually blend in oil; add remaining ingredients and mix well. Makes about ¾ cup dressing.

Poppy Seed Dressing

Try this unusual dressing on a fruit salad or a green salad with citrus fruit. When you make a salad of citrus fruit with greens, be sure to add the fruit to the greens with the dressing just before serving, for greens wilt quickly when combined with citrus fruits.

⅓ cup honey
1 teaspoon salt
2 tablespoons vinegar
1 tablespoon prepared mustard
¾ cup salad oil
1 tablespoon finely chopped onion
2 to 3 teaspoons poppy seed

In a small bowl, combine the honey, salt, vinegar, and prepared mustard. Gradually add the salad oil, beating thoroughly until the mixture is very well blended. Stir in the onion and poppy seed. Turn into a pint jar, cover, and chill for several hours before serving to blend the flavors. Shake well before mixing in the salad. Makes about 1¼ cups dressing.

Avocado Salad Dressing

Make this salad dressing ahead and store it in a tightly covered container. It will keep for about a week without darkening or losing flavor.

1 cup mayonnaise
2 green onions, cut up
2 tablespoons lemon juice
1 teaspoon sugar
¼ teaspoon garlic powder
1 medium-sized avocado, peeled, seeded, and diced

Combine mayonnaise, onions, lemon juice, sugar, and garlic powder in an electric blender; whirl until thoroughly mixed. Blend in avocado. Store in a tightly covered jar in the refrigerator. Makes 1½ cups.

Blender Salad Dressing

Try this dressing on cole slaw, grated raw carrots, sliced cucumbers, or mixed greens.

¼ cup salad oil
¼ cup whipping cream or evaporated milk
1 tablespoon vinegar or lemon juice
½ teaspoon salt
1 teaspoon dill weed
1 small clove garlic, peeled
1 or 2 grindings pepper
2 teaspoons prepared mustard

Combine in your blender the salad oil, whipping cream or evaporated milk, vinegar or lemon juice, salt, dill weed, garlic, pepper, and prepared mustard. Whirl until smooth. Makes ½ cup dressing.

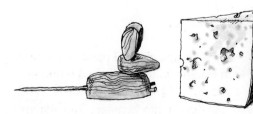

Garlic-Egg Dressing

This salad dressing especially complements citrus flavored green salads. It thickens like mayonnaise when beaten, but changes to the consistency of French dressing when used on greens. Try it on a green salad to which you have added avocado slices and orange or grapefruit sections.

1 clove garlic, peeled and sliced
¼ teaspoon prepared hot mustard
1 teaspoon salt
1 teaspoon sugar
3 tablespoons cider vinegar
¾ cup salad oil
1 egg (at room temperature)

Put the garlic clove into a mortar with the mustard, salt, and sugar; mash and blend thoroughly with a pestle. (Or mash the garlic and blend in the mustard, salt, and sugar.) Stir the vinegar into the mashed seasonings, then pour into a bowl. Add the salad oil and break in the egg. Beat with a rotary beater until thickened. Serve immediately or store in the refrigerator where it will keep well for several weeks. Makes about 1⅓ cups.

Piquant Dressing

This light dressing goes well with most green salads. It's especially delicious with the Green Salad, Smörgasbord Style, on page 11.

1 cup salad oil
⅓ cup wine vinegar
¼ cup dry white wine
1½ teaspoons Worcestershire
3 or 4 drops liquid hot-pepper seasoning
1 tablespoon brown sugar
1½ teaspoons salt
1 teaspoon paprika
¼ teaspoon coarse black pepper
1 clove garlic, peeled

Combine all the ingredients in a covered pint jar. Shake until very well blended. Set aside several hours or overnight before using. Discard garlic. Makes 1½ cups.

Mayonnaise

Try this recipe when you need a basic mayonnaise dressing for a salad.

2 egg yolks
1 teaspoon salt
1 teaspoon sugar (optional)
1 teaspoon dry mustard
  Dash of cayenne
2 to 4 tablespoons lemon juice or vinegar
2 cups salad oil

In a deep bowl, thoroughly mix the egg yolks with salt, sugar, mustard, and cayenne. Stir in 2 tablespoons lemon juice or vinegar. While beating briskly with a rotary beater, start adding the oil, a few drops at a time. Beat well after each addition until about ½ cup of the oil has been added. Beat in the remaining oil, adding it about 2 tablespoons at a time. Makes about 1 pint dressing.

Blender Mayonnaise

One speedy way to make your own mayonnaise is with the blender. This basic mayonnaise and the five recipes that follow are specifically designed to be made in the blender. A basic instruction to keep in mind is to have the lid on the blender whenever you turn it on. Once it is running, you can remove the lid to pour in the salad oil.

2 tablespoons lemon juice
½ teaspoon salt
1 teaspoon prepared mustard
1 egg
1 cup salad oil (or part olive oil)

Combine the lemon juice, salt, mustard, egg, and ¼ cup of the oil in the blender. Whirl at high speed until smooth. Remove top and slowly pour in the remaining oil, and continue to whirl until thick, about 2 or 3 minutes. Makes about 1½ cups.

Chutney Mayonnaise

Serve Chutney Mayonnaise on fruit salad or spread on fruit bread. First make mayonnaise as directed above; then stir in 2 to 4 tablespoons prepared chutney and whirl about 2 minutes longer, or until smooth. Makes about 1½ cups.

Curry Mayonnaise

Curry mayonnaise is especially good with artichokes, or makes an excellent binder for rice, meat, or seafood salads.

Make as for mayonnaise above, except reduce the amount of mustard to ½ teaspoon and add 1 teaspoon curry powder, or more if you like a stronger curry flavor. Makes about 1½ cups.

Green Mayonnaise

A pleasant way to begin a dinner is to serve a seafood salad with Green Mayonnaise.

8 sprigs water cress
6 to 10 spinach leaves (depending upon size)
5 sprigs parsley
  Boiling water
1¼ cups mayonnaise
2 teaspoons lemon juice

Place water cress, spinach, and parsley in a bowl and cover with boiling water. Let stand 6 minutes; drain and rinse in cold water. Put water cress, spinach, and parsley in the blender; add mayonnaise and lemon juice. Whirl until smooth and evenly colored. Makes about 1½ cups.

Horse-Radish Mayonnaise

Here is an excellent dressing for sliced tomatoes, seafood salads, or hard-cooked eggs. Simply add 2 tablespoons grated prepared horse-radish to 1 cup mayonnaise.

Russian Dressing

This dressing is delicious with green, vegetable, egg, or seafood salads.

To 1 cup mayonnaise, add 2 tablespoons chili sauce, 2 tablespoons finely chopped pimiento or green pepper, ½ teaspoon vinegar, and ½ teaspoon paprika. Mix well. Half a hard-cooked egg, chopped fine, and 1 tablespoon chopped chives may also be added. Makes about 1½ cups dressing.

Anchovy Mayonnaise

Use this mayonnaise to dress fish, vegetable, and green salads. Make mayonnaise as directed on page 90. Add about 6 anchovy fillets or 2 tablespoons anchovy paste; whirl about 2 minutes longer or until thoroughly blended. Makes about 1½ cups.

Egg Mayonnaise

Serve this mayonnaise with fish as a sauce, or use it to bind fish, meat, or vegetable salads.

Make mayonnaise as directed on page 90. Add 1 hard-cooked egg and ½ teaspoon instant minced onion and blend until smooth. Makes 1½ cups.

Green Goddess Salad Dressing

Use this dressing on greens or shellfish salads. Make mayonnaise as directed on page 90. Add 3 anchovy fillets, 1 tablespoon chopped green onions, 2 tablespoons chopped parsley, 1½ teaspoons dried tarragon (or 1 tablespoon fresh tarragon), 1½ tablespoons chopped chives, and 1½ tablespoons tarragon vinegar. Stir in with a spatula; then whirl until smooth. Makes about 1½ cups dressing.

Creamy Roquefort Dressing

This dressing is one that keeps well in your refrigerator, so you may want to double or triple the recipe. A good combination of greens for this dressing might be equal parts of romaine, red leaf lettuce, and endive.

½ cup mayonnaise
¼ teaspoon dry mustard
¼ teaspoon monosodium glutamate
⅛ teaspoon salt
   Dash freshly ground pepper
½ teaspoon Worcestershire
   Few drops liquid hot-pepper seasoning
3 ounces Roquefort cheese, crumbled (about ½ cup)
   About 1 tablespoon water

In a bowl combine the mayonnaise with the mustard, monosodium glutamate, salt, pepper, Worcestershire, and hot-pepper seasoning; stir until well blended. Add the crumbled cheese and mix to distribute evenly. Add water to thin the dressing to the consistency you prefer for salads. Keep in a covered jar in the refrigerator. You may wish to add a little extra water when you use the dressing after it has been chilled. Makes about 1 cup, or enough for about 6 quarts of torn greens.

Green Goddess-Yogurt Dressing

Like the traditional dressing, serve this low-calorie version of Green Goddess Dressing with greens, especially romaine, and with combinations of greens and cooked shellfish or chicken.

    1 teaspoon crushed dried tarragon
    2 tablespoons tarragon wine vinegar
    1 small green onion, minced
    1½ tablespoons minced parsley
    2 teaspoons anchovy paste or finely chopped
        anchovy fillets
    2 teaspoons sugar
    ½ teaspoon salt
    1 cup low-fat yogurt

In a bowl, soak tarragon in tarragon wine vinegar for about 5 minutes. Add onion, parsley, anchovy paste, sugar, salt, and yogurt. Stir until well blended. Makes about 1¼ cups (about 10 calories per tablespoon).

Avocado Dressing

Serve this low-calorie dressing on cabbage salads with fruit or vegetables. It will keep its clear green color for several days in the refrigerator.

    1 medium-sized fully ripe avocado
    1 small onion, peeled
    ½ cup sour cream
    2 tablespoons lemon juice
        Dash pepper
        Dash liquid hot-pepper seasoning
    1 teaspoon salt

Peel and cut the avocado directly into an electric blender; cut in the onion and whirl until smooth. If you don't have a blender, mash the avocado with a fork and finely chop the onion; combine them in the small bowl of an electric mixer. Add sour cream, lemon juice, pepper, liquid hot-pepper seasoning, and salt; whirl or beat until smooth. Makes about 1⅔ cups.

Low-Calorie Blue Cheese Dressing

This dressing is especially easy to make if you have a blender. Serve it on greens or vegetable salads.

    1 cup low-fat cottage cheese
    ½ cup buttermilk or skim milk
    2 tablespoons white wine vinegar
    ½ package blue cheese salad dressing mix

Combine in your blender the cottage cheese, buttermilk or nonfat milk, white wine vinegar, and blue cheese salad dressing mix. To measure the dressing mix, empty the package into a small custard cup, then spoon out half of it. Whirl until smooth. Refrigerate. If you like a thinner dressing, stir in milk or buttermilk when you use it. Makes 1½ cups (about 12 calories per tablespoon).

Thousand Island-Cheese Dressing

This dressing contains only about 13 calories per tablespoon. It can be used on fish, meat, vegetable, or green salads.

    1 cup chive cottage cheese or low-fat cottage cheese
    ¼ cup buttermilk or skim milk
    ½ teaspoon grated onion
    3 tablespoons pickle relish
    2 tablespoons catsup
    2 tablespoons vinegar
        Dash liquid hot-pepper seasoning

Combine in your blender the cottage cheese and buttermilk; whirl until smooth. Turn into a bowl and stir in grated onion, pickle relish, catsup, vinegar, and liquid hot-pepper seasoning. Makes 1½ cups dressing.

Creamy Fruit Dressing

A small amount of currant jelly makes this dressing light pink in color and gives it a tang that complements melons, berries, or almost any fresh fruits.

1 small package (3 oz.) cream cheese
1 cup (½ pint) heavy cream
1 tablespoon lemon juice
  Pinch salt
¼ cup currant jelly

Mash the cream cheese, gradually stirring in 2 tablespoons of the cream and the lemon juice until well blended. Add the salt and currant jelly, and mix in well. At this point the mixture might be covered and chilled in the refrigerator until time to serve.

Just before serving, whip the remaining heavy cream and fold in the cheese mixture. Use as a dressing for fruit salads or as a sauce on fresh fruit desserts. Makes about 2 cups dressing.

Apricot Cream Dressing for Fruit Salad

Refrigerate this dressing until ready to serve over fruit salad. It will last for several days if kept covered and refrigerated.

1 package (3 oz.) cream cheese
2 tablespoons milk
¾ cup apricot purée, sweetened
1 tablespoon lemon juice
¼ teaspoon salt

Soften cream cheese with a fork. Add milk and blend until smooth. Combine cream cheese mixture with apricot purée, lemon juice, and salt; beat with an electric mixer or whirl in an electric blender. Refrigerate until ready to use. Makes about 1 cup.

Honey-Mint Dressing

If low-fat yogurt is used, this dressing contains only about 15 calories per tablespoon. Serve it on any fruit combination or on a green pea salad.

½ cup plain or low-fat yogurt
1 tablespoon mild honey
2 teaspoons finely chopped mint or dried mint
1 teaspoon lemon juice

In a bowl, stir together the yogurt, honey, mint, and lemon juice. Makes about ½ cup dressing.

Creamy Honey Fruit Dressing

Pass this dressing separately to spoon over fruits cut in generous chunks. Taste the dressing, and if you prefer it even more tart, add more lemon juice.

1 small package (3 oz.) cream cheese, softened
2 tablespoons honey
3 tablespoons lemon juice
½ teaspoon grated lemon peel
¾ cup salad oil
  Dash of cayenne
  Salt

Beat together until smooth the cream cheese, honey, lemon juice, and lemon peel. Add oil very slowly, beating after each addition, gradually increasing amount of oil as mixture thickens. Add cayenne and salt to taste. Chill. Stir well before serving. Makes about 1⅓ cups.

Orange Custard Sauce

Serve this creamy orange sauce to dress fruit salads. It is especially good with papaya in combination with such fruits as oranges, pineapple, and strawberries.

2 eggs
2 tablespoons mild honey
2 tablespoons lemon juice
3 tablespoons sugar
⅔ cup orange juice
½ teaspoon grated orange peel
⅛ teaspoon salt
½ cup cream

In the top of a double boiler, beat the eggs lightly; beat in honey, lemon juice, sugar, orange juice, orange peel, and salt. Cook over hot (just under boiling point) water until slightly thickened; cool. Whip cream until stiff and fold in. Makes about 2 cups.

Honey Dressing

The mildly sweet flavor of this dressing blends with both fruit and vegetables.

1 cup salad oil
½ cup catsup
⅓ cup vinegar
⅓ cup honey
1 teaspoon salt
1 teaspoon paprika
1 teaspoon grated onion
1 whole clove garlic

In a mixing bowl or the small bowl of your electric mixer, place the salad oil, catsup, vinegar, honey, salt, paprika, and grated onion. Beat thoroughly with a rotary beater, or beat at medium speed on your electric mixer until very well blended. Add the whole clove of garlic, and let stand about 10 minutes, or until you are ready to use it. Beat again just before serving, and remove the garlic when it has flavored the dressing to your taste. Store in your refrigerator, beating every time you use it. Makes about 2½ cups.

Cottage Cheese Salad Dressing

This has fewer calories than most salad dressings, but is high on flavor. Use it to dress mixed greens and vegetable salads.

½ cup large curd cottage cheese
½ cup skim milk
1 teaspoon salt
¼ teaspoon freshly ground black pepper
2 tablespoons lemon juice
¼ cup chopped green pepper
¼ cup chopped green onions
1 small clove garlic

Combine in an electric blender the cottage cheese, milk, salt, pepper, lemon juice, green pepper, onions, and garlic; whirl until smooth. Makes about 1½ cups dressing.

Orange and Cheese Dressing

This low-calorie dressing is good on fruit salads or on shredded carrot or cabbage salads with fruit.

1 cup chive cottage cheese or low-fat cottage cheese
2 tablespoons orange marmalade
¼ cup buttermilk or low-fat milk
3 tablespoons lemon juice

Combine in your blender the cottage cheese, orange marmalade, buttermilk, and lemon juice. Whirl until smooth. Makes about 1¼ cups (about 17 calories per tablespoon, using chive cottage cheese and buttermilk).

Index

Photographers: Ernest Braun, page 70; Clyde Childress, page 15; Glenn Christiansen, pages 8, 9, 11, 17, 18, 20, 30, 36, 38, 42, 47, 50, 85, 86; Darrow M. Watt, pages 4, 14, 24, 25, 46, 48, 49, 51, 56, 60, 64, 68, 69, 74, 75, 76, 78, 82, 84. **Cover photograph by** Glenn Christiansen; recipe on page 47, Summer Shrimp Salad. **Illustrations by** Earl Thollander.

96   Index